WITH PATIENCE AND FORTITUDE

WITH PATIENCE
AND FORTITUDE

A Memoir

CHRISTINE C. QUINN

wm

WILLIAM MORROW
An Imprint of HarperCollins*Publishers*

All insert photographs appear courtesy of the author, except page 4 (*bottom*): Steven Macauley; page 5 (*middle*): Dan Luhmann; pages 10 and 11: White House photos; page 12 (*top*): Spencer Tucker; pages 12 (*bottom*), 13–16: William Alatriste.

HarperCollins books may be purchased for educational, business, or sales promotional use. For information please write: Special Markets Department, HarperCollins Publishers, 10 East 53rd Street, New York, NY 10022.

FIRST EDITION

Designed by Jamie Lynn Kerner

Library of Congress Cataloging-in-Publication Data has been applied for.

ISBN 978-0-06-223246-5

13 14 15 16 17   OV/RRD   10 9 8 7 6 5 4 3 2 1

To Mary Callaghan Quinn and
Anthony L. Catullo Jr.,
two people who knew New York
City was always home

CONTENTS

WITH PATIENCE AND FORTITUDE

PRELUDE

When I was a kid, I fell in love with libraries. I loved the silence. I loved the smell of the books, and the hushed sounds of people stepping from room to room. It was always exciting to check out books at the librarian's desk and to clutch them in the crook of my elbow as we left. Biographies of people who changed the world were everything to me.

I still love libraries, and for me the two lions that sit on either side of the steps of the main branch of the New York Public Library at Forty-second Street and Fifth Avenue are dear friends. I watch them and imagine their moods and feelings. I think about their reactions to the events that crown our city, and the attacks that harm it. For me, the lions symbolize both my aspirations and those of my city.

Patience and Fortitude, they are called. Mayor Fiorello

La Guardia gave the lions their names during the Great Depression. He knew our citizens would rise to the occasion, and to spur them on, he named the lions. La Guardia was known for his passions for the poor and the powerless. He brought energy and hope to our city, when it was mired in the Great Depression. That's another reason I love the lions.

And then there's Father Mychal Judge, the chaplain of the New York City Fire Department who died in the attacks of September 11. He rushed into the command center of Tower One, and when the second tower went down, he died. Many New Yorkers remember the picture of Father Judge's body being carried out of the building. It still brings tears to my eyes. I learned that when he was low, he would walk up Fifth Avenue from his rectory and stand across the street from the library and look at the lions and pray for patience and fortitude. Whenever I think about Patience and Fortitude, I find myself thinking about him and his good works—with the poor, the homeless, people with AIDS, and anyone else who was struggling to get by in difficult circumstances—and how patience and fortitude served him well in his work.

I love those lions. They make me think of La Guardia's endless energy and hope, of Father Judge's faith and courage.

I may not be famous for patience. I like to get things done, done on time and done right. And New Yorkers on the whole are an impatient lot. We run across the avenue when the traffic light turns yellow, and we check our watches when a line moves slowly. The tempo of our city is fast and exciting.

I find myself exhilarated by it. The energy fits my personality. So patience is something I try for, but don't always achieve.

But when it comes to fortitude, we can't be beat. That energy that has us tapping our toes when a subway is slow—that's the same energy that makes us get up in the morning and accomplish whatever we need to do. That's the energy that built our skyscrapers and attracted the artists, the writers, the performers. That's the energy that fuels every immigrant community in our town, from the settlers of New Amsterdam to the people who live in all our boroughs today, in all the amazing variety of their cultures and languages. And that's what has sustained me through my life.

Most of us don't have it easy, and neither did I. We encounter difficulties that call for patience, and we face obstacles that demand fortitude. That's life, and that's the story of my life, just as it may be the story of yours. But we keep on trying to make it through, somehow, with hope for patience and trust in our fortitude.

During the holiday season, Patience and Fortitude are often bedecked with beautiful holly wreaths around their necks. I love the dressed-up lions. They make me stop and think of all the things we can celebrate in this magnificent town of ours, and they remind me of the work that is still to be done and the fun that is still to be had.

So I have a ready answer to the unfortunate politician's question "Who is your favorite New Yorker?" I always say that I have two favorites, Patience and Fortitude.

PART I

Growing Up Quinn

CHAPTER 1

Quinns in the Suburbs

My mother gave wonderful parties. She hated living in the suburbs, but she loved entertaining. She kept a bag in the credenza in the dining room that was filled with place cards for every occasion. There were place cards decorated with drawings of the *Niña,* the *Pinta,* and the *Santa Maria* for Columbus Day; George Washington's head for Washington's Birthday (that was before they combined Washington's and Lincoln's birthdays into a single national holiday); and wreaths for Christmas. You name the holiday, she had a set of place cards for it.

One year she threw a Mickey Mouse party for my birthday. It was Mickey and Minnie, all the way. The house was festooned with Mouse stuff, and my mom sent me around the neighborhood so I could give all the kids who were invited mouse ears to wear and a long black shoelace for a tail. Another year was the Raggedy Ann birthday party—my mother *loved* theme parties. And it wasn't just for kids. Her New Year's parties were famous. The entertaining dwindled around the time I was six, but she did give one last New Year's Eve party when I was in seventh or eighth grade. In an attempt to replicate the Times Square ball drop, she strung netting along the ceiling of the playroom and filled the netting with balloons, which cascaded down at the stroke of midnight. The parties stopped completely when she became too ill.

A great hostess, she was also a terrible cook. I mean terrible. Still, I was her eager helper. Usually that meant going with her when she picked up takeout, but on occasion she would cook, usually out of a can. Every vegetable I ever had at home, aside from iceberg lettuce, was canned. I recall once suggesting to my mother that we follow a recipe for tomato sauce that appeared on the back of a ketchup bottle, which I thought would be better than just getting the sauce out of a can. It wasn't half bad, so my mother decided to save the recipe. And she used it often, reading the recipe off the back of the bottle she had saved. I loved helping my mother. We adored each other from the very beginning.

My sister remembers watching my mother and me preparing this "homemade" spaghetti sauce. I was maybe eight years old, standing side by side with my mother at the stove, which was nothing unusual because I was always at my mother's side. I was on a step stool so I could reach over the pot and pour jars of ketchup into it. The ketchup went all over the kitchen, but nobody cared.

My dad tells a story about her cooking when they were first married. Shortly after the wedding, my parents invited the priest who had married them over for dinner. My mother asked my father, "How do you make a roast beef?" He said, "Oh, it's easy, you just put salt and pepper on it, and roast it for a couple of hours at 350, and you're good to go." (My father didn't have any sisters, so he and his brother had helped in the kitchen.)

So my father came home from work, and my mother was in the bedroom—which was in the back of their apartment—getting ready, and the kitchen was filled with smoke. She hadn't taken the meat out of the wrapper or put it in a pan. She just sprinkled salt and pepper on the outside and put it in the oven at 350 degrees, as instructed (or at least that's how my father tells the story). They took the priest out to dinner. She was a terrible driver, too, and she hated driving.

Cooking and housekeeping—which my mother also loathed—and driving the car were what suburban motherhood was all about. This was a problem. Throughout her life, she was a die-hard city person. She missed the city. She felt isolated. She despised housework and gardening. Although my father adapted better to the suburbs, he missed the city as well. He never stopped talking about his magical childhood on Ninety-sixth Street and First Avenue, which was not such a great neighborhood when he was growing up, a rough part of town, but he loved it and still tells endless stories about the neighborhood as if it were paradise.

So why did my parents choose this suburban life? In part because it was what people were doing in that era, and in part because in the late 1950s it wasn't so easy to find an affordable apartment for a middle-class family in a good neighborhood in Manhattan. That's what pushed people to the suburbs. It still does. My parents wanted a nice home for the family—this was well before I was born, but my sister, Ellen, was around. So without doing much planning or research, they opened up the *New York Times,* saw an ad for a development in Glen Cove, Long Island, and got in the car to investigate.

They found a house on a dead end. It was a classic four-bedroom, center-hall colonial, with a two-car garage on an acre of land. My mother was sold on it without much looking around because in her mind dead ends meant no cars and lots of space for children to play safely. Libby Drive would be perfect.

It was for me. You could be out all day after school and into the long summer evenings. We would play baseball (with a tennis ball) or basketball, ride our bikes, or just run around. Lots of the neighbor families had kids, and I knew everyone, so there was no need for playdates or other arrangements.

I just went outside and looked for the other kids. I'm told that I was very good at organizing the other kids, so I came to be known by the adults as the Mayor of Libby Drive. My mother loved this aspect of our life, and she extended her love of party favors and planning to other parts of the neighborhood children's lives. For holidays like Halloween, she would make personalized candy bags for all the neighbor kids. But not just any candy. Before the holiday, she would determine what each child's favorite was—and that would fill the bag, personalized by favorite and by name. Presenting each child with their own bag brought her such joy.

The one thing missing from my perfect childhood was a dog. It took a while for me to discover why I couldn't convince my parents to get me one. It turns out that my sister, Ellen, who is ten years older than I am, did have a dog when she was little. She was named Dolly the Collie. Ellen also had another pet, Daisy the Duck. Dolly the Collie and Daisy the Duck would go around the neighborhood together, and sometimes Daisy would ride on Dolly's back. When Ellen was out playing with the neighborhood kids, Dolly would go looking for her and herd the children into a pack as if they were sheep. Then Daisy would waddle in and join them.

Unfortunately, one day some of the children resisted Dolly's herding and she nipped them, the way collies herd sheep. This was not good. Then at some point a raccoon ate Daisy the Duck. And soon afterward Dolly got sick and had to be put down. So none of it ended well, and my father refused to get another dog. It was, to quote my father, "a debacle." In response, he has adopted the position that he's not supportive of living things, from plants to puppies, in a house. (He's careful not to include children in that group.) I wasn't around for Daisy and Dolly, but their story epitomizes the funny and highly unique aspects of my family—when things were going well. It also fairly explains the edict against dogs.

Ellen was ten years old when I was born. The family had been in the suburbs since she was two. I came as a surprise. In that era women had their babies young, and there weren't a lot of women who got pregnant at forty. My mother was excited and a bit embarrassed. I think it probably also came as a shock to Ellen. It had taken my parents five years to have her, and when my mother didn't get pregnant in the years that followed, they'd just assumed that more children were not in the cards, although it was never open for discussion. They just didn't talk about such matters. But when my mother knew I was on the way, the conversation turned to the choice of my name.

Tradition dictated that I had to be named after a family member, and my parents settled on Julia, after my aunt and my maternal great-grandmother. For some reason, my sister objected. My father tells me that Ellen was already upset that she would have to share my mother with a baby, after ten years of having her all to herself. So in an attempt to make

Ellen feel better about her new sister, they let her pick my name.

The story goes that Ellen chose Babe, after Babe Didrikson, a famous Olympic athlete and golfer. (She was also a lesbian—was that prophetic?) Ellen had been reading about her and liked the name. Babe Quinn? That didn't go over too well with my mother, who suggested that she try again. So Ellen decided to name me after Christine, a girl who lived across the street, and whom my mother wasn't that fond of. And since my mother was "sick of Quinn, Quinn, Quinn," as my father says, I was given my mother's maiden name, Callaghan, as my middle name. Christine Callaghan Quinn. My sister chose the first name, my mother the second, and the third was my father's. This triumvirate was the central core of my childhood. Even though Ellen was a lot older, she was my friend and protector.

My father worked as an engineer at Sperry Gyroscope, which was only twenty minutes by car from Libby Drive. My father was a veteran of World War II. He served in the navy in the Pacific. After the war, like millions of other veterans, he used his GI Bill benefits to get an education. He went to college and graduate school. He became an electrical engineer and spent the next thirty-two years at Sperry (which became Sperry Rand and, later, Unisys Corporation). In that day, each specialty had its own union, and my father was shop steward for the electrical engineers.

My dad's union responsibilities meant the world to him,

and three times in his life he had to go out on strike. I think one reason he cared so much about his union was that his father, who had been a streetcar operator on Sixth Avenue in Manhattan, was a proud member of the TWU (Transit Workers Union). Years later I learned that before the streetcar operators had a union, they had to get to the garage at least an hour before the cars were due to go out. You wouldn't be guaranteed a streetcar to drive until you got there, and if all the cars were taken, you didn't work that day. When the union came in, it changed all that. (You'll get to know my father, Lawrence Quinn, as you read this book, but just for starters, he is a smart man who has dedicated his life in different ways to the service of others. He may not show much emotion in a traditional way, but he demonstrates it by showing up every time he's needed for support and strength.)

Although Ellen named me, we couldn't have been more different. She was skinny and had strawberry blond hair and a classic Irish complexion. My mother always said that when I was born I looked like a Butterball (as in, one of those round frozen turkeys), and Ellen looked like a chicken. I had tons of that Irish black hair and was chubby. Ellen remembers that when our mother brought me home from the hospital, I was so alert that she half expected me to stick out my pudgy little hand, shake hers, and introduce myself.

Our physical differences didn't go unnoticed, and as I grew up, my father never hesitated to joke about how there are two types of Irish bodies. He would say that my sister,

Ellen, looked like the famine had never ended. And that I would have married well in Ireland because I'd have been helpful on the farm. He'd say, "You're big-boned. You would have been good back in Ireland in the fields flipping sheep."

Mommy made no secret of the fact that she hated her upper body and was always on a diet. She thought she was fat, but she didn't have the faintest idea how to lose weight. Here's an example of her idea of a diet: we'd go to Burger King, and she'd get a Whopper and have just half the bun. One time when I was in elementary school, she put me on a doctor-supervised diet. I'd go once a week to get weighed. That made sense. And then if I lost weight, I'd be rewarded. That sounds good, in theory, but my reward was an ice-cream cone that I could eat on the way home. See what I mean?

Things were a bit disorganized in the house. It just wasn't my mother's focus. Keeping things in order wasn't a priority for her. For example, if you were looking for scissors and tape, you'd never find them in the same drawer—you were lucky if you found them at all. Dinner at the Quinn house was almost always determined by the route home from the last lesson of the day. If it was ballet in Port Washington, for example, we passed Burger King or Roy Rogers on the way home, so it would be Burger King or Roy Rogers for dinner. I guess it's no surprise that my kitchen skills are less than stellar, although I recently taught myself to bake. I like baking because you follow the recipe, you do what you're told, and it largely works out.

My mother, who as I've said hated to drive, spent much of her day behind the wheel of our car taking us for lessons. Glen Cove and the neighboring towns at the time offered a lot of chances for lessons. When I was just a month old, my mother started schlepping me with her in the car. She laid me in a laundry basket in the backseat and tied the basket's handles to each of the doors. "You went everywhere with us," Ellen told me. "One time I turned around, and you were standing up in the basket." The first time I ever stood up was in that basket in the backseat of the car. For the first few years of my life, I was just along for the ride, picking Ellen up and dropping her off. And then when I was three or four, it started for me, too.

Long before the concept of overscheduled children existed, my mother had us rocketing around. We took every lesson she could find: horseback riding lessons, swimming lessons, diving lessons, French lessons, ballet lessons, and ice-skating lessons. Then there were the painting classes, pottery-making classes, and an array of nature courses in the summertime at the Cold Spring Harbor Lab. (That's what sparked my sister's interest in geology.) Sometimes we'd have several in one day.

My mother would pick me up at school, and then in the car I'd change out of my Catholic school uniform and into my horseback riding clothes. Then after that lesson, off came the blue jeans and on went the ballet leotard—all in the back-seat of the car. (It's a skill that has come in handy in my life as Speaker of the City Council—sometimes I have to go to five different events in a day. While going from a parade of some kind to a public hearing and then to a political dinner, I often have to change in the back of the car. The only difference is that now I also have to put on makeup while the driver is navigating New York City streets and traffic. One lesson I quickly learned is never try to put on eyeliner while the car is moving. I do it anyway.)

Whether I liked the lessons or not, I had to go to them. I loved the nature classes, and I liked painting. My father's apartment is still full of paintings that I made when I was in elementary school.

What I liked best was going to the stable. I started riding when I was four and rode until I went to college. When I was growing up on Long Island, horseback riding was available to just about everybody. Stables were all over the place, and the lessons were not very expensive. At first we rented a school horse, and then when I was in junior high school, they bought me a horse of my own. My first horse was named Classy. I loved her. And then I got Arthur, my second horse. I would take lessons year-round and then go to local horse shows, where I got to compete against other riders.

In summers, when I was old enough, I spent the whole day at the stable. It was like going to camp. Whether I rented a horse or had my own, I had to be at the stable almost every day to ride it and later take care of it, so I learned what it meant to be responsible for another living creature. I also learned about doing physical work in all kinds of weather, because no matter the weather, you still had to take care of your horse. And I really liked the other kids who hung around at the stable. It was great being around a big gang of people who were all working on the same thing.

Ellen had her own horse when she was little, too. My parents, in a typically well-meaning but ill-informed fashion, had bought her a failed racehorse. The horse was so small my parents called her Little One. Actually, if you shaved her hooves, she was just a big pony. Racehorses are trained to run, not to carry little girls, so the first thing Ellen's horse did was buck her off and break her nose. Ellen had that small horse—or pony—for quite a while.

You might think my father was making an executive salary to be able to afford all these lessons and extras for his daughters. That wasn't the case. My mother's family subsidized much of it. My mother's sister, Julia, lived with her parents (until she moved into our house, along with my grandmother, when I was in fourth grade). She was a bookkeeper at a department store, and since she lived at home she didn't have to pay rent, buy food, or pay a lot of bills, so she used her money to splurge on Ellen and me.

Ellen and I had more lessons than the rest of the kids in the neighborhood, but as I was growing up, my mother began to apologize because I didn't get as many lessons as

Ellen did. She worried that I was not well-enough prepared for life because of that. I couldn't understand what she was talking about. I remember thinking, "More lessons? There aren't enough hours in the day!" That was before I knew she was ill.

I always wondered what my mother's obsession with lessons was all about. She would pick me up and drive me around from place to place even when she was clearly not feeling well or was very tired. When I was six, she was diagnosed with breast cancer. Ellen just recently told me that after the diagnosis, our mother's primary goal was to see me through grammar school. I wonder if she ran herself ragged because she knew she didn't have much time. Perhaps that was part of it. But it's hard to know because she had done the same thing with Ellen. My mother was determined that her daughters would succeed at whatever we decided to do.

Her mission in life was to make her daughters well-rounded, independent women: women who would have many skills and lots of experiences. This made it possible for us to have conversations with all kinds of people about all kinds of things. I'm grateful for that gift to this day.

She had been a career woman before Ellen was born, working for Catholic Charities as a social worker, a job she loved. She majored in biology in college at Mount St. Vincent's, and her plan was to become a doctor. But that wasn't possible. The demand for places in medical schools from veterans returning from the war made it improbable that a woman like my mother would be admitted. This was a time when working women of all sorts stayed home, and many of them moved to new houses in the suburbs. Despite this disappointment, my mother respected doctors and held them in high regard, making sure we always had the best medical care. To this end, she developed an interview, or grilling, technique that allowed her to find out everything about a doctor—from their college GPA through the ins and outs of their specialty training. It served her well.

Mommy left work in 1956, when Ellen was born. My father's job was to provide for the family, and he took great pride in that role. My mother's job was to be a mother and take care of the house. But she didn't give up on trying to have an impact on the world around her, even if it was limited to helping people in the neighborhood. She believed strongly in the importance of helping people—or, if you put it in a religious framework, which I think she did, corporal works of mercy or living the beatitudes.

Whenever there was an injustice in the neighborhood, Mommy took care of it. Ellen remembers, "She had this ridiculous trench coat with excessive jewelry on it, and whenever anything required her attention in the neighborhood, she would grab her trench coat, head out the door, and whatever the problem was, she'd get it resolved." For example, we had Italian neighbors who didn't speak English; she would go with them to the school over and over, to help their kids get the services they needed.

Although she really wanted to, going back to work was not in the stars for my mother. It frustrated her terribly. In the years before she died, she was trying to teach herself typing so she'd have a better skill set when she started looking for a job. She had a typewriter on her desk and next to it was a self-instruction book called *How to Type*. She was frustrated and angry that she didn't get to do the things she wanted to do. Angry that she was sick. Angry that she was scarred. Angry that her life didn't turn out the way she'd hoped. Just thinking about all her sorrows makes me sad for her.

In the end, I believe my mother wanted Ellen and me to have all the things that had eluded her. She wanted us to be able to do whatever we wanted in life. And when we figured out what we wanted to do, she expected that we would do it exceedingly well. My mother would be pleased to know that both her daughters wound up doing things we love. And we've both worked to be the best we can at what we do.

CHAPTER 2

Being Irish

Growing up in Glen Cove, I knew that my family was different from the other families in our neighborhood. First of all, my parents were much older than my friends' parents. Today a woman having a child at age forty is not uncommon, but these were the postwar years, when women married young and had their babies right away. Second, my sister and I were ten years apart. Most of my friends had brothers and sisters around the same age, so they played together and went to the same school at the same time. I was eight when Ellen went away to college. It wasn't bad, just different.

But most important, we were the only family on the block with live-in relatives. If this had been the Bronx or Queens or just about any neighborhood in Brooklyn where immigrants lived, it probably wouldn't have been in the least bit odd. But in Glen Cove, as in many postwar suburbs, the nuclear family was the rule. Mother stayed home, Father worked, and there were usually no more than two children.

I was in fourth grade when my mother's father died and my grandmother and my mother's sister, Julia, moved in with us. You would think that the addition of two people to our household would have changed our home life in significant ways, but it didn't, in large part because both my grandmother and my aunt were quiet and kept to themselves, and also because they had always been involved in our family, even before they moved in. My grandmother tried desperately not to bother anyone, and to anybody who knew her, she came across as meek and mild. She must have been in her eighties when she moved into the guest room, and I remember my parents and everyone talking about how they expected her to wither away and die after my grandfather's death because he was supposed to be the strong one whom she relied on. But despite her mild nature, she was capable of rising to the occasion when her life was on the line.

Her maiden name was Nellie Shine. Her married name was Nellie Callaghan, and it's entirely unclear how old she was, but at some point in her teen years she came to America. She was poor. She and her family had lived in Newmarket, County Cork, in Ireland. She came to New York because her parents had died, and her eldest sister had taken in an orphan from the village, and there simply wasn't enough money for all of them. Her sister told Nellie that she had to go to America to be with her brother and her cousin. So she got on the next available ship—which happened to be the *Titanic*.

Notwithstanding "women and children first," more first-class men than third-class girls got off the *Titanic* alive. My grandmother was one of those girls. She was once quoted in a book about the Irish on the *Titanic*. When she was asked, "How did you get out?" she said, "When the other girls dropped to their knees to pray, I took a run for it." Once I rather cheekily said to a priest, "I guess my grandmother knew there was a time for praying and a time for running." He, quite wisely, said, "No, Christine. Your grandmother knew you could pray while running." I think that's exactly what happened on that day, and also during those days in Glen Cove after my grandfather died. It is a great metaphor for the struggle of all immigrants and for the city of New York.

I didn't know about my grandmother's place in history until my mother told me. And my mother only found out by accident when she was in the eighth grade. Her class had a lesson about the *Titanic*, and they read the *New York Times* account of the disaster. My mother came home from school that day and said, "Mom, it's so strange. We read a story in the *New York Times* about the sinking of the *Titanic*, and there was a girl on the ship with the same name as yours, Ellen Shine." My grandmother said, "No, that was me."

It's an Irish thing. My grandmother never spoke a word to me about escaping the sinking ship, and our mother forbade Ellen and me to ask her anything about it. I'm guessing that the primary reason she didn't talk about it was that she'd been traumatized by the experience. I don't know this from her directly, but many years later, when she was in a nursing home and suffering from dementia, I would visit her, and she would scream, "Get in the boat! Get down! He has a gun!" In eyewitness accounts of the ship's sinking, there are reports of ship's officers shooting men who tried to rush the lifeboats despite the strict order that women and children should be the first to board. I felt terrible that she relived the most frightening experience of her life over and over again. But there was nothing we could do to keep her from thinking that she was still in a lifeboat on the night of April 15, 1912.

As I said, when my grandmother moved in with us, my mother's sister, Julia, came with her. She'd never married, and she lived at home with her parents, so when my grandfather died, it just made sense that both she and my grandmother would come to live with us. Aunt Julia moved into my sister's room, and then whenever Ellen came home to visit, Julia stayed in my room, which had two beds. Julia had never lived on her own. She was exceedingly generous, but she was not particularly independent or strong. She was even quieter than my grandmother, and I had very little real communication with her. It's difficult to know the reason: maybe because she was a simple and somewhat passive person, or maybe because she was mostly deaf—or both.

My aunt and mother both developed progressive hearing loss, starting in late high school. They never knew why, but my father's theory was they had some kind of viral infection or they had lead poisoning from the paint in the apartment where they grew up. By the time I was born my mother's deafness was pretty far advanced, but she could still hear the television if it was turned up really loud and talk on a special telephone, at least until she became totally deaf. There was a light over the phone that flashed when the phone rang, and there was a volume control that let you amplify the sound.

If you didn't know it, you couldn't really tell my mother was deaf except for a bit of a speech impediment. I never noticed it at all, but other people commented on it. She also had trouble with words she hadn't learned before she went deaf, like *Parmesan cheese,* which she called "paramecium cheese." She loved Burger King, but she couldn't say *Whopper;* she called it a "whooper."

The biggest change that came in the wake of my grandfather's death, beyond my aunt and grandmother moving in, was the end of our summers at Rockaway Beach. For my mom's whole life, my maternal grandparents had rented half of a two-family house or a bungalow close to Rockaway Playland, an old amusement park that's long gone. Rockaway is a barrier island off the coast of Queens that was long popular with working-class New Yorkers. In those days, before the urban renewal programs of the 1960s and 1970s leveled huge sections of the Rockaways, people would rent these tiny bungalows on narrow lanes for the summer. The women and children would go out for the whole season, and the men would join them for weekends or commute to the city every day by subway. We went out for the day, for a weekend, or for weeks at a time.

We'd spend most of the day at the beach, although the waves were often too big and the tide too strong for a young child to go swimming. The adults brought hot tea in Thermoses—very Irish—and we'd all have crunchy sandwiches for lunch (crunchy because of the sand that invariably got into them). Then we'd go back to the bungalow, where my grandfather was always cooking these huge pieces of meat. Having been a firefighter, he was a very good cook, which probably explains why my grandmother and my mother were so terrible in the kitchen.

My grandfather was a very big guy, and he'd stand over the stove, enveloped in smoke, wielding an enormous chef's knife that his brother had given him. He'd make hams and steaks and roast beef or pot roast. The bungalow would feel like it was 9,000 degrees, and we'd have this huge dinner, which was the last thing we wanted to eat after a day at the beach. It was hot even without the cooking, and no one had air-conditioning. After dinner we went to the amusement park or to one of the arcades and almost always got ice cream.

In the summer, we'd also have barbecues in Glen Cove and other parties, especially before my mother got cancer but sometimes after, too. Mommy would invite extended family, many of whom were police officers. At these events, my grandmother would again show the quick thinking she wasn't always given credit for. In those days most police officers carried their guns all the time. So, since there would undoubtedly be drinking at the parties, my grandmother was concerned. Her solution was to stand at the front door holding a dresser drawer and making everybody put their guns into it. Then she would lock up the drawer and tuck the key into her bra. At the end of the evening, she would decide who was sober enough to get their gun back.

My grandfather Callaghan, who only had a third-grade education, started out in America as a milkman, then became a firefighter and rose to the very high rank of battalion chief in the New York Fire Department. When La Guardia was mayor, part of my grandfather's job was to pick him up and drive him around to watch the big fires. La Guardia loved the firefighters.

When my grandfather retired, he opened a liquor store in the Bronx not far from where my grandparents lived in Inwood, a neighborhood at the northern tip of Manhattan. I often visited their apartment, and it is one of the ways I came to love New York City and why I moved to Manhattan as soon after college as I could.

On some of my visits, my grandparents took me shopping at the now-long-gone Gimbels department store in Herald Square and to see Julia, who worked there as a bookkeeper, and get her employee discount. But what Pa liked best was taking me shopping for Mary Janes at a neighborhood shoe store. Pa loved these shoes, and got them for me in every conceivable color. Mary Janes are low-cut leather shoes with a little strap across the instep that's fastened with a buckle or button. They have a rounded toe box, a very low heel, and a thin sole. They're totally appropriate for a little girl for dressy occasions, especially when they're made of patent leather.

From my grandparents' house in Inwood, I'd walk hand in hand with this giant of a man to his car, and we'd drive over a bridge to a shopping district in the Bronx, where we'd go to the same shoe store again and again.

The problem was, the shoes never fit me. I have a low anklebone, and the way Mary Janes are made, they would cut into my ankle and I'd wind up with blisters. It didn't matter when I was really little, but as I got older I hated wearing them because they hurt. But Pa loved these shoes—and for him, getting his granddaughter fancy party shoes was a mission. Blisters or not, he believed they were essential. Getting party shoes for a little girl clearly meant more than just a fashion statement.

Working in Gimbels, buying Mary Janes—the Callaghans had an affinity for shopping. And it wasn't lost on my mother—she was a championship shopper. She had tons of stores she loved—each one had a different specialty for her, a different reason we went there. We would spend hours looking, trying things on, discussing items—sometimes buying but not always. And always eating in the store's restaurant for lunch. They had great names. Lord and Taylor's was the Bird Cage—it was filled with colorful fake birds and birdcages.

She had some particular tastes. In the age of panty hose, she was a nylons-and-white-gloves gal. Forward-thinking in some ways but old-fashioned in others. In the 1970s she and I would search and search for stores that carried stockings—it was a quest.

My mother also loved to shop for my father. Recently, somebody complimented him on his dashing outfit. He opened up the jacket, and there was a Saks label. He was still wearing a jacket she had bought him thirty years ago! My father also still wears the navy overcoat my mother bought him for his father's funeral in 1970.

My father's father, Pa Quinn, died when I was four, and my father's mother, who I called Nana, had only a few more years of good health after he died before she entered a nursing home. Both of them were born in Ireland. My grandfather, Martin Quinn, was born in 1894 in County Clare and came to New York in 1913. My grandmother, Ellen Lancer, came from Schull, which is in West Cork, sometime around 1911 or 1912, joining her sister, who was already here. Both of them worked as domestics.

Nana's first job was with a family that lived in a brownstone on the Upper West Side. Then she went to work as a chambermaid for a wealthy family in Oyster Bay, on Long Island. At the time she met my grandfather, she was working as a lady's maid for a family that lived in a house between Fifth and Sixth Avenues, around where Rockefeller Center is now. My grandfather was a streetcar operator on Sixth Avenue (and then later a bus driver, after the trolleys were put out of service). No one knows exactly how they met—it wasn't the kind of thing they talked about—but in all likelihood Nana met Pa Quinn while riding a streetcar he was driving.

Nana was a tough cookie—smart and in charge—which you had to be when you were a lady's maid, the second-highest rank for a female servant, just below housekeeper. (*Downton Abbey* fans, take note.) She had a lot of responsibilities. She traveled through Europe two or three times with the family she worked for. Along the way she picked up a working knowledge of some of the foreign languages she heard.

The Quinns were married in 1924, and after having their two boys, Lawrence and Martin, who they nicknamed Buddy, they moved to Hell's Kitchen, a neighborhood just north of where I live now. It was full of Irish immigrants who worked, among other jobs, on the Hudson River docks loading and unloading cargo ships. My father tells me that one of my grandfather's uncles, Uncle Mike, had a saloon on Ninth Avenue somewhere between Thirty-eighth and Forty-fifth Streets.

Soon they moved to Yorkville, and my father grew up on East Ninety-sixth Street. When my father, Lawrence, was five, Nana took him and Buddy to Ireland for two years to look after her dying mother, or at least that's how the story went. It could have been true, but it's also likely that she and my grandfather had a fight and she took off. Nana drank too much and had a tendency to just take off.

She knew how to take charge. During World War II, Nana used the German she'd learned while traveling in Europe to help a family in their neighborhood—Yorkville had a large German immigrant population. One of her German neighbors came to the Quinns' door asking Nana for help because the FBI was threatening her with deportation. Nana accompanied her to the FBI office, and between her little bit of German and the neighbor's little bit of English, they were able to sort things out, and the German family stayed in New York. That story makes me think my father married a woman very much like his mother.

Nana was tough enough to deal with unpleasant or tragic realities head-on. So when my father enlisted in the navy in World War II, her reasonable expectation was that he would die in the war and never return. This prospect was personally horrible, but it also had some practical implications—such as what to do with my father's clothes. Nana sent them all to be altered so they would fit Buddy, his younger brother who was shorter and chubbier. So when my father came home from the war he had no clothes! What she had done was tragic, sad, practical, and Irish. She was Irish, so why would she expect the best outcome—that my father would survive the war? And why waste his clothes?

By the time I was born, my grandparents had moved from Ninety-sixth Street to a two-family house on Sedgwick Avenue in the University Heights neighborhood of the Bronx. After Pa Quinn died and before Nana's health declined, I would visit her there. She was still tough as nails and very smart. She definitely wasn't a cuddly grandma, but she was very attentive and focused and spent a lot of time with me. When I visited, she'd take out an old purple metal Louis Sherry candy box that was full of little flags from all over the world. We'd dump them out on the couch, and she'd teach me the flags of all the nations. She was so proud—she knew them from all her travels. She would quiz me over and over and beam with pride when I got the nations correct.

Given that all four of my grandparents came from Ireland, you might think I'd have lots of stories about what their lives were like before coming to America. But while Ireland was often a topic of conversation at family gatherings and dinners, none of my grandparents talked about their life in Ireland with great specificity, and they didn't talk about *being* Irish. They *were* Irish, so that was a given. And while they were proud of their Irish heritage, as am I, they were much more focused on becoming Americans. Both my grandfathers served in World War I, which was how they got their citizenship. It's not the only reason they served, but it was important to them to become American citizens.

Think about it: my grandparents were just four kids who got on ships and left behind the only homes they had ever known. They had no expectation that they were ever going to return, from a place they had never even seen. But they had heard about this place—New York. They had heard that unbelievable things could happen here, that there was something great, almost mythical about this place. So they came here. And they were prepared, as immigrants always are, to work hard, to do whatever it took, and that's what they did.

They were servants or car washers or milkmen or firefighters or bus drivers. They worked as hard as they had to, and New York gave them a great opportunity, through that hard work, to have homes that they could live in, and some of them eventually die in. All four of their children went to college. Some of their children even went on to graduate school. All their grandchildren went on to college and became professionals. And that's because they decided to take the risk and come to and believe in New York.

My grandparents' stories helped me enormously in understanding the experiences of most New Yorkers. People's ethnicity matters. It's part of who they are. It mattered to my parents and grandparents because even though they wanted to be Americans and New Yorkers, they didn't want to forget the past or set aside their cultural heritage, which they valued. For my family, that meant taking pride in having persisted and persevered in the face of devastating poverty. Their heritage is fueled by faith and enriched by literature and poetry. We've learned to find beauty in everyday things, even in the face of misfortune. And although we've come to expect the worst, that doesn't keep us down or prevent us from simultaneously striving for the best.

I've found that all New Yorkers—whether they came here from someplace else or had parents or grandparents who did so generations ago—share an appreciation that you can leave where you came from and bring big parts of it with you and find something wonderful in a place you've never been. Immigrants built the city that welcomed my grandparents. They had no money and they didn't have much education. But they came with energy, faith, loyalty to their family, and determination to make good lives for themselves and for generations to come. New York City provided the rest—opportunity, obstacles, and a sense that anything was possible. That's the city they loved, and the city that Kim and I are proud to call home.

CHAPTER 3

Our House of Sorrows

I can still see the classroom. I was in eighth grade. My friend Debbie and I were sitting at our desks. The chairs and desks sat two by two in rows, with aisles on either side. Debbie leaned over to me and whispered, "Can you believe Sister so-and-so said you're going through a hard time because your mother has cancer? Isn't that crazy?" Debbie said that the sister had told her mother and asked her to tell Debbie to be nice to me. That wasn't necessary. Debbie was already my friend.

I don't know if I was going through a hard time just then, but my mother had taken a turn for the worse. She was often sick and not always around, but this was the first time anyone had mentioned the word *cancer* to me. When I got home from school, I called my sister and told her what I'd heard. Ellen said it was true. While I wasn't entirely shocked, because things never seemed right with my mother, I was still surprised to be hearing it for the first time.

I now know it was not the first time Ellen actually told the truth. This is how it happened. Our mother had scheduled her mastectomy and arranged for her parents to come out and stay with us. She didn't tell them why she needed them until they arrived, and when she did, my grandfather started crying. Ellen, who was sixteen at the time, was outside the room, listening. No one told her what was going on, but she figured it out from what she overheard. Ellen, a very smart and determined girl, decided that someone had to tell me why our mother would be gone for so long.

She took me upstairs to the one large bathroom in our house. I remember that bathroom vividly, with its icky tan-orange tiles and fixtures and matching paint. I liked to take baths there, and when I was older I'd hang out there because it was quiet and the lock on the door guaranteed privacy. I'd soak in the tub and read magazines and books, which is something I still like to do.

Ellen sat me on the edge of the porcelain tub and locked the door. She told me that our mother was sick and explained she had cancer and would be going to the hospital for an operation. I asked Ellen if Mommy was going to die. She said that she didn't know.

To this day, I remember everything about that room, including what it felt like to sit on the edge of the tub. Yet as much as I've tried—and I've really tried—I can't remember that conversation with Ellen. My mind goes blank. Maybe it was too much for me to absorb. I was six. So that's why I was surprised when Debbie said my mother had cancer. But my conversation with Ellen goes a long way toward explaining why I had this sense throughout my childhood that something was wrong without knowing exactly what. Children usually have a way of knowing when something is up, and I knew something was way off kilter.

There were definitely clues. For one thing, my mother had enormous scars from the mastectomy. That kind of procedure was even more brutal in the 1970s, and there was no such thing as reconstructive surgery. So to hide her scars, she always wore men's button-down shirts (another clothing item we searched for on our shopping missions), which was weird because none of the other mothers dressed like that. Occasionally you could see the scar if her nightgown or housecoat slipped. To cover when anyone noticed, my parents told this ridiculous story that she'd had a tooth infection, which had spread down her face and into her chest area, and that the scar was a remnant of the infection. Of course it was absurd, but I never thought to question the story, maybe because I wanted to believe it.

I can't blame my parents for not being more direct. They were doing the best they could, at a time when people knew next to nothing about child psychology and the best way to talk to a child about something as serious as the likelihood that her mother was going to die. And they would never have sought professional help. That wasn't even in the realm of possibility. This was an era when people kept secrets from their children and didn't ask for help in dealing with their troubles. Some people took to drink, as my mother did and as others in my family had done. Others took to prayer, as my mother, aunt, and grandmother did. But one thing they all did was keep it from the children.

In addition to the scars and the excuses that made no sense, my mother would periodically disappear for a week or two. Usually while she was away getting treatment, I'd get sent to stay with family friends who had moved from Glen Cove to Maryland. I really liked and missed them, so it was fun and I didn't think anything of it. I was thrilled to see them. Other times the stories got crossed, leaving me confused. For example, on one occasion, when my mother was supposedly in the city taking care of her friend Marge, who I was told was sick, my sister said that Mommy was in the hospital. I didn't know if that meant she was at the hospital looking after Marge there, or if they got in a car accident together and were both in the hospital being treated for their injuries. Somehow I knew not to ask, so I was left to imagine all kinds of things.

It took me many years, and some therapy, to understand that I did what children typically do in a situation where there's an ill parent, and especially when the illness is not discussed. You wind up assuming that you're somehow responsible, even though what's going on around you is reasonably beyond your control. You come to believe that it's your fault that your mother isn't feeling well. Or you think you've been sent away because *you* were bad, even though you can't figure out what you've done wrong. And then you go about trying to fix things, which for a child is a terrible psychological burden, because the truth is that it's all beyond your control when you're a child and you really can't fix anything.

I like to think, after years of working on understanding it, that one of the good things that came out of this terrible experience was an unexpected and positive legacy. Because of what I lived through, I'm highly motivated to fix things, to get things done. And unlike when I was a child, I really *can* fix things and make them better—for my family, my friends, and the people I serve. I really doubt I would have become the first woman—or the first LGBT person—to be elected Speaker if I hadn't been driven by a leftover sense of guilt and responsibility for my mother's illnesses and her absences. It never would have happened. If I were given a choice, I'd have found a different motivation, but I don't have a choice, so there's no point going down that road.

Finding out from Ellen that I had already known that our mother had cancer helped me clear up something of a mystery. Maybe *mystery* is too strong a word. But it's helped me better understand something I wrote for a Mother's Day essay competition for the *Record-Pilot,* which was Glen Cove's local weekly newspaper. I got second place for my tiny essay. It was even published. There's no date on the clipping, which my mother framed and kept in the living room (I still have it), but I'm guessing I was around nine years old. The title was "My Mom":

> *My mother is marvelous. She is sweet, kind, and always there when I need her. I can't dream of living without her. Even when she is sick we're first on her list. Though sometimes we take her for granted, she never takes us for granted. She is always showering her love over my family with a bright and cheerful smile.*

I can't dream of living without her. I may have forgotten what Ellen told me about the severity of our mother's illness, but I had been thinking about what it would be like if something ever happened to her. And it's clear from what I wrote that I couldn't imagine it.

My mom soldiered on for years. As her strength waned, her moods darkened. Alcohol was always her drink of choice, but as the pain worsened, she was given lots of medication for that and the stress. The doctors did what they could for her, but the meds and the drinks made for some fuzziness and unpredictability. If my guilt over not being able to fix her was painful but in the end provided useful motivation, growing up with a mother who sought solace in drink, with all its pain and suffering, gave me another strength.

This situation caused me to be a watcher—to gauge my mother's moods and reactions and plan my response. So now I often can tell from body language how someone is feeling, and even when I was a little girl, hanging around at parties my mom gave, I learned to size up a room full of people in an instant. Psychologists now name it social intelligence or emotional intelligence, but back in the day, I just had this sixth sense that developed from worrying about how my mother would be acting or feeling. It probably was one reason the grown-ups called me the Mayor of Libby Drive, and it helped me get through many situations in my life. It was a small blessing, but I don't take it for granted, and I am grateful.

In seventh and eighth grade I began organizing protests. When I was in seventh grade, the school wouldn't provide band uniforms for us. I knew the school had the uniforms because when we were in the lower grades we had marched in them. So I organized an ill-fated, unsuccessful band boycott of the Memorial Day parade. And then in seventh or eighth grade, with a couple of other kids, I organized a letter-writing drive to try to keep the deacon in the parish from being transferred. It failed, too. But these failures didn't deter me. They whetted my appetite.

When it came to my schoolwork, my mother kept close tabs on my grades. I'd bring home a test, and she'd ask, "Was your grade the highest?" There were a couple of kids in the class who were smarter than I was, and she'd always ask, "What did so-and-so get?" She wasn't asking to make me feel bad; she was trying to motivate me. I know that because when it came to a big test or the science fair or the art fair, she'd do her best to temper my expectations and let me know that it was okay not to get the highest grade or win first place.

I think she was particularly sensitive to my feelings about these things, because Ellen was an academic star and I wasn't. Ellen went on to Franklin & Marshall College, where she majored in geology; she did her master's in geology at Harvard and has an MBA from Rensselaer Polytechnic Institute. And she is extremely successful and superhardworking. (To this day, the family joke is that Ellen is the good daughter because she went to Harvard and married a doctor.)

But for all these years, the activity that sustained me was horseback riding. If you have ever looked into the eyes of a horse, you know what I mean. Sadness and kindness flow from them. And if you take care of your horse almost every day, you form a relationship that is filled with gratitude and affection. And a horse is reliable. You don't find them happy one day and miserable the next. An apple, a carrot, a sugar cube, and all is well. I found in the stables not only solace but the need for commitment and a kind of control that I couldn't find elsewhere.

If I'd had any idea that the summer of 1982 was going to be my mother's last, I'd have chosen another time to break my back. But that's the thing about trouble. You don't see it coming, and then you just have to make the best of it.

In all my years of horseback riding and competing, I'd never had a serious accident. But one Sunday, as I got a leg up onto my horse, he reared up, and I fell off onto a rock. In seconds my father and our cousin, Father Gene, who was visiting from Ireland, were standing over me while an EMT was checking my vital signs and telling my dad he was calling an ambulance.

Out of the corner of my eye, I could see my dad was in a panic. He had reason to be. He said, "You can't take her to Stony Brook Hospital. I have to take my wife to Sloan-Kettering in the morning, and my mother-in-law's checking into Glen Cove Hospital. I can't have three of them in different hospitals." So the EMT said, "Either you take her to Stony Brook, or I have you arrested for endangering the life of a minor."

By this point in my life, I had no problem challenging authority and taking charge. I'd seen my mother question doctors endlessly, grill them about where they went to school, and challenge their recommendations for treatment. So when the EMT said we had no choice, I decided we did have a choice. But looking back and considering the very real possibility that I was seriously hurt, I see that the EMT was right. From the perspective of a sixteen-year-old who had to get home to help take care of her mother and grandmother, there was only one option. I couldn't be in the hospital with everything else that was going on and definitely not in a hospital that was an hour and a half from home. I looked up at the EMT, who was straddling me, and yelled, "Get off me or I'm gonna knee you in the balls!" I think he was so shocked by what came out of my mouth that he did exactly what I told him to do. (Given how angry I was, I can easily imagine that what I said was laced with profanities.)

Somehow, with a little help from my father and my cousin, I got up off the ground, and after a few tentative steps I felt mostly okay. We walked the horse a bit to make sure he hadn't hurt himself, put him in the trailer, and drove back to Glen Cove. My father went in to tell my mother that I'd been in an accident. I heard her scream as I slowly climbed the stairs and tried to get into bed. I got one leg up onto the bed, but that was as far as I got because it hurt too much to lift the other one. I called for my father and asked him to pick up my other leg and put it in the bed, which he did. It hurt like hell, and I screamed. The EMT had been right. I needed to go to the hospital.

After examining me and taking X-rays, they checked me in. It turned out I'd fractured three of my vertebrae. When you crack vertebrae, they put you in bed for a few days and wait to see if you begin to heal. It helps to be young, and in a couple of days I was sent home and told to get a lot of rest, and not to do any lifting, riding, or anything strenuous. After I got home, my summer didn't include the recuperating that had been suggested. It involved looking after my mother and grandmother.

This may not have been the best recuperation plan, but it's what had to be done, and I was home anyway. And whether I was physically ready or not, it's what I wanted to do. In the morning, after my father left for work with my aunt—he drove her to the train station so she could go to her job at Gimbels—I'd make sure my grandmother was awake and I'd get her going. Then I'd head downstairs to the family room, where we had a hospital bed set up for my mother, to make sure she was awake. I'd give her the morning pills.

Once my grandmother was dressed, I'd put her in a chair in the driveway to wait for the bus to take her to the Glen Cove Senior Center, where she spent the day. She really enjoyed her time at the center—it gave her a place to go and something to do—and I think it contributed in no small part to her longevity. Next I'd get my mother out of bed and make her breakfast. After breakfast I'd get her set up in the backyard, where she liked to sit. Then I did the laundry, cleaned the house, made lunch, and gave my mother her afternoon pills.

After lunch my grandmother came home from the senior center, and I'd take care of her for a while. Then it was time to make dinner for both my grandmother and my mother and give my mother her later-in-the-day pills. And once I was finished with my grandmother and my mother, I'd get dinner ready for my father and my aunt. In the evenings they would generally take over my mother's and grandmother's care, and sometimes I'd go to a friend's house for the night.

Or I'd head upstairs and talk on the phone with my friends or watch TV.

For most of the years after my mother's first surgery, which she'd had at our local hospital, she was treated in Manhattan at Memorial Sloan-Kettering Cancer Center. But over that last summer, she got too sick to continue going in and out of the city, and her treatment was moved to North Shore Hospital on Long Island, a terrific hospital. They had this amazing service, where a van with doctors and nurses and all the necessary equipment would come to the house to give my mother chemo or whatever treatment she needed right at home. It made things a lot easier for her and for me and my dad.

The first time the North Shore van arrived, a social worker came along to do a formal intake. My father and I sat next to each other on the sofa in the living room, and the social worker sat diagonally across from us. He asked a long list of questions including, "Is the patient depressed?" We said she was. (She was dying—of course she was depressed!) And then he asked, "Is the patient suicidal?" My father said no, which was true. My mother wanted desperately to live at that point.

At the end of the intake interview, the social worker offered family and individual counseling. We both said no almost instantaneously. I wasn't the kind of person to talk about my feelings easily and never have been, and back then I didn't see any need.

Ellen was extremely helpful during all this. We talked all the time about what was going on and what needed to be done. She came home often to do anything and everything. I never really mentioned being upset. I don't think I even had the language or the sense of what I would express. Besides, I was focused on the tasks at hand. That was easier than thinking about the fact that my mother was going to die, and it gave me a sense of purpose and control. Counseling would never have worked for my father. He would never talk about his feelings with Ellen or me—let alone a stranger. I followed his lead for my own reasons.

When the summer was over, I went back to school, and we had to get nurses during the day. That was something of a relief to me, but by this stage of my mother's illness her hearing was even worse, and she decided I was the only person whose lips she could read. So I was the one who could be her go-between. I remember her saying, "Only Christine can tell me. I can only hear Christine." It's true that she could read my lips more easily than anyone else's. Sometimes people tell me that when I talk, I move my jaw and mouth in an exaggerated way. I think it came from those years of talking with my mother so she could read my lips and understand what I was saying.

Those last months of being my mother's go-between were a nightmare. When there was a medical decision for her to make or unfortunate news to be delivered, I more often than not had to be the one to talk with her. She was back and forth between home and the hospital and basically bedridden at this point because the cancer had spread to her bones and so her hips were mostly hollow. She couldn't understand why she wasn't allowed to get up, and I was the one who had to explain that her bones were too weak to support her and that if she put any weight on her hips, they'd crumble. There was nothing but bad news, so I had to tell my mother, in slow increments, information that ultimately made her realize that she was dying. By that stage, the doctors had nothing else they could do and my mother was waiting for a miracle.

All she had left was prayer. She had an altar set up on her bedroom dresser, with lots of relics and religious statues. All the statues represented women, and the relics came from women. Elizabeth Ann Seton was her favorite saint. It wasn't lost on me that every entity my mother prayed to was a woman. She believed in women to bring her miraculous intervention. She would say the rosary. And when she couldn't take the time to say a whole rosary, she'd say prayers. I found her faith hard to accept. As I witnessed her painful decline, I didn't think we would get a miracle.

My mother had survived for so long that when the end came, in late December, we were caught off guard. She hadn't been doing well, but she hadn't been doing well for a long time, so we convinced ourselves she had at least a few more months. Now of course I know, but I couldn't have then, that when I left for the stable for two hours on the afternoon of December 21, she had only hours to live.

When I got home she was barely conscious. She couldn't talk. Her eyes were open, but she didn't seem to see us. And her breathing was labored. The nurse who was there recommended we get her to the hospital, and my father and I agreed. We debated calling 911 or calling a private ambulance: a call to 911 would mean she'd get taken to the local hospital, which we knew she didn't like. So we called for a private ambulance to take her to North Shore.

I was sitting at the kitchen table waiting for the ambulance to get there when I heard through the closed louvered doors to the playroom, "Oh no!" I don't know who said it—my father, Aunt Julia, or the nurse—but I ran up to my room crying. I came out a few minutes later to go to the bathroom and saw my father at the bottom of the stairs looking up at me. I guess he'd been on his way up to tell me. I noticed he was wearing a red plaid shirt and an Irish sweater, which was odd for two reasons. First, my mother had bought matching red plaid shirts for herself and my father, and he was wearing the shirt, which he never wore. Second, it wasn't at all cold in the house, so I didn't know why he was wearing a sweater.

My father had tears coming down his face, and I asked him a question that really didn't need an answer. I said, "Is Mommy dead?" And he said, "Yes." I didn't wait for him to come up the stairs—I just headed to the bathroom. When I got back to my room, I called my sister, who wasn't home, and I left a message with her fiancé that she had to come home right away. Then I called a high school friend and made plans to spend the night at her house. I was ready to leave by the time she came to get me, and as we left the house, the ambulance was just arriving.

As devastated as I was that my mother had died, I wasn't sorry that she died before the ambulance arrived. At that stage of her illness, the hospital could have done nothing other than extend her life for a few hours or days, which would have been torture for her.

The funeral was held on Christmas Eve at McLaughlin Kramer and St. Patrick's in Glen Cove, the same place where we later had my grandmother's and my aunt's funerals. Not long before she died, my mother had given Ellen an envelope with all manner of instructions. She'd already made her own funeral arrangements, picked out her coffin, and prepared her funeral card. In the instructions, she told Ellen what clothes she wanted to wear and asked that the coffin be closed. She cared very much about how she looked, and the ten years she'd spent fighting cancer had taken their toll. It turns out, however, that Julia wanted an open casket. As my sister, Ellen, recently observed, "We had a distraught live lady who wanted it open. And a demanding dead lady who wanted it closed." Julia won that argument. We had an open casket.

The funeral card my mother designed was not your typical mass card. It was printed on cream-colored wedding-invitation card stock. A gold Celtic cross adorned the front on top. In the middle was a quote from Saint Paul, with his name underneath. When you opened the card, it said on the inside, "Gratefully, Mary Callaghan Quinn, December 21st, 1982." It was printed in such a way that Saint Paul's name on the outside of the card lined up perfectly with the date of my mother's death on the inside, so when the card was closed, Saint Paul's name sat directly over the date.

I stayed fairly well composed during the wake's three sittings, but I lost it at the funeral. Even before it started, I remember my father and sister walking up to the front of the room to pray at my mother's casket. I was standing in the doorway in the back and couldn't move. I watched from behind as Ellen turned to my father, crying, "Oh, Daddy." I must have joined them at some point, because I remember the coffin. I'd already said no to the funeral director when he'd asked me if I'd bring the wine and the host up to the priest during the mass. I'd pointed to my first cousins and said, "They'll do it!" I just couldn't.

It was a typical funeral mass, which is similar to a regular mass: two readings, a gospel, and a sermon. There were two priests doing the mass. One came from my family's church, St. Patrick's, and one came from St. Rocco's, a church that my mother liked and attended on occasion. The priests both gave eulogies as well. No one else spoke, which was typical in those days for Catholic funerals.

I had to be taken out of the funeral at one point, because I was so upset. My mother's friend Mrs. Gorman (the mother of the family I was always sent to visit) walked me around outside. One of my friends said later that since I'd held up so well at the wake, she was surprised when I fell to pieces at the funeral. I begged my father and Ellen to let me skip the cemetery. It was such a long drive, and I just wanted to go home and go to bed. But I had no choice. When we got there, we watched as the plain wooden box was lowered into the ground. The coffin was inside the box to protect it from the dirt.

The priests recited some prayers, we were each given a rose to throw on top of the coffin, and then it was over. Everything went off as my mother had planned, except for the open casket and the fact that we ran out of funeral cards. She hadn't counted on the huge number of people who would attend. We also didn't have a gathering at our house or at a restaurant after the funeral, which is typically done, because the funeral was held on Christmas Eve; people had other places to go and things to do.

After the burial, I couldn't wait to get home, but Ellen had other ideas. She wanted to finish the Christmas shopping and insisted that we go home, change, and drive to the Miracle Mile shopping area in Manhasset, which isn't far from where we lived. What I didn't know at the time was that among the notes our mother left for Ellen were instructions regarding Christmas gifts. The note listed the gifts she'd already bought and the ones she wanted Ellen to buy, and she explained where they were supposed to go, including which ones were for me. In the instructions she wrote, "This gift is for Christine," and each time she wrote my name, she underlined it three times. Ellen thinks she did that because she wanted to be sure that I received the gifts she'd bought for me.

I can't remember what I got for Christmas that year, but I know what I got from my mother. She left me with a sense of worth and possibility. She left me with a sense that I have a responsibility to continue her mission, to improve people's lives, and to make sure that nobody is left behind. The urgency she conveyed—because she knew her time was short—gets me up and out every morning. My mother taught me to use every minute, because we never know when our time is up.

CHAPTER 4

High School Follies

Our house was a much quieter—and sadder—place at the start of 1983. My mother was gone. My grandmother, too. She had moved into a nursing home before my mother died. Her age and related conditions made it too difficult for us to take care of her. So now it was just Julia, my father, and me living at home. Without any discussion, we quickly fell into our own routines and very much went our separate ways. For me that meant focusing on school and school-related activities, spending time at the stable, and going out with my friends on the weekends.

That sounds sad, and it was, but there were a lot of bright spots for me in those years. I loved high school, Old Westbury School of the Holy Child. It was a place of salvation and great comfort for me in many ways. It hadn't been my first choice—I'd wanted to go to a coed public high school—but that wasn't in the cards. My mother and father were both extremely religious, so there was never any question that Ellen and I would go to Catholic school. At my high school, being Catholic was a given, but it was background noise to me. You were taught the way things were, and you weren't expected to ask questions.

What made Holy Child so special was the fact that it was a small school: there were only twenty-four students in my entire class, and they were all girls. A small school was a great place for me, especially after my mother died, because everyone was so supportive.

Because there were so few of us, we got a lot of individual attention, and no one fell through the cracks. Everyone participated in every aspect of school life, including the sports teams, because you needed everybody to play. So there wasn't the kind of hierarchy you might have found at a larger school. We did have cool kids, smart kids, and athletic kids, but our classes were so small that nobody cared.

My experience with a single-sex high school was also positive. When you take boys out of the equation, girls wind up focusing on their potential and their skills. I think if every girl went to a girls' school, regardless of ability to pay, it would be an extremely empowering experience. It certainly was for me.

Also, the emphasis on reading—from the very beginning

of my Catholic education right through the Great Books course I had in high school—gave me a lifelong passion for libraries. (In my role as an elected official, I've always been a big advocate for keeping libraries open and protecting them from budget cuts. In my early years as City Council Speaker, when there was a budget surplus, we restored funding so that libraries could stay open six days a week instead of five.)

I'm not a fast reader, so it takes me longer than most to finish a book. But I loved the way we learned. Our teachers were terrific. Our classes were interestingly structured. We had a marvelous program in our junior and senior years that put English, history, and theology together under Area Studies. They were team-taught by the three separate departments. One year you did Europe. The next year you did the United States. They put the juniors and seniors together. We had great literature classes. Some of our classes were held in the convent, so we would sit on couches and comfy chairs and listen and talk. That place probably gave me the best sense of confidence about my intellectual abilities.

In grammar school, I had loved reading the biographies of great political and civil rights leaders like Eleanor Roosevelt, and Franklin Delano Roosevelt, and John F. Kennedy, and Bobby Kennedy, and Martin Luther King Jr. I learned so much from biographies of nonpoliticians who did important things, like Helen Keller; Booker T. Washington; George Washington Carver, who was born a slave and became a leading botanist; Molly Pitcher, who fought in the Revolutionary

War; Marie Curie, who discovered polonium and radium; and Dr. Charles Drew, who discovered plasma. Those biographies got me hooked on politics and government, which I came to love. I saw the evidence that one person could have a positive impact on the world. The biographies also inspired me to want to do something—and to maybe even be the first at something—that made a difference in people's lives.

Academics and reading weren't the only inspiring parts of high school for me. For example, you might not think that organizing Sports Night at Old Westbury was the beginning of a life in politics, but I was one of the lead organizers, and I loved it. Lots of schools did it. Some call it Sports Night, but others call it Color Night. Half the school was the blue team, and half the school was the white team, and we had themes. So you'd have to do an entrance that was on the theme, and a dance, and cheerleading, and there'd be athletics. People would work on Sports Night for months. You either did it perfunctorily or you got totally into it. I got totally into it.

My freshman year the theme was "The Wild, Wild White West," because I was on the white team. Another year it was a mythology theme, and another it was "The Great White Way." My father always jokes that between the political demonstrations I organize, which can include costumes and thematic signs, my professional career is just an extension of Sports Night. I loved the group activity of it. I actually loved every big activity in high school. I was editor of the newspaper and senior class president—not such a feat in a class of twenty-four. But we had fun both in school and out-side. And I had my own car, which made getting to school and going out on weekends a lot easier.

I had all the freedom a teenager could want, probably too much. My father never set a curfew—I came and went as I pleased. I don't think he was prepared for raising a typical teenage daughter, especially since my sister hadn't gone out a lot when she was in high school. And now that my mother was gone, he was thrust into this role that he had no frame of reference for. In the generation in which he grew up, it was the wife's job to set the rules and keep tabs on what the children were doing. I didn't always make it easy for him, and I don't think he was always happy about the things I chose to do, but he never said a word.

Aunt Julia, who still lived with us, financed my social life in the kindest manner. She devised a way to be my unofficial banker. I didn't have a formal allowance, so whenever I needed money, I'd go to her underwear drawer. She kept a statue of the Virgin Mary in the drawer, and inside the statue was a place where she'd stash bills. She always made sure there were plenty of twenty-dollar bills there, so if I needed cash, I'd take twenty or forty out of Mary. Julia must have checked regularly, because the statue always held what I needed.

My friends and I traveled in packs, mostly, and we had

fun. This part of life is when many teenagers start drinking. On a typical weekend, a group of us would go to Manhattan to the Limelight or the Palladium. Or when we stayed on Long Island, we'd go to Malibu in Lido Beach or to TR's (for Teddy Roosevelt) in Williston Park. We'd go out around nine or ten and meet up with other friends. Sometimes one or more of the girls would bring along a boyfriend or an older brother. Then you'd just go and hang out, dance, and drink. If you weren't driving, you'd drink until you were drunk. It certainly wasn't sophisticated, but getting smashed didn't seem out of the ordinary, at least among the people I knew. We'd sometimes make our way home at three or four in the morning.

From early on I assumed that I wasn't going to have a romantic life. I just wrote it off. So when my friends talked about boys they liked, the ones they found attractive, and which ones they were going to pursue, it felt irrelevant to me. I had my own philosophy, my own set of goals. I was going to make something of myself. I was going to help people. I was going to have fun. But as far back as I can remember, I subscribed to the belief that you can't have everything. I had friends, I was smart, and I did pretty well in school, and that was enough. I didn't worry about my sexuality. I didn't feel much of anything. I had a couple of dates with boys, and they didn't work, so I went back to the group and put all other thoughts out of my mind.

My friends and I were a close-knit group, and the fact that there were no boys romantically in my life didn't bother me at all. What bothered me was being what I believed was overweight and unattractive. My sadness and my lack of physical self-confidence meshed together, leaving me feeling powerless and desperate to fix this aspect of my life. I had failed to make my mother better. I had given up on romance. I had to succeed at losing weight. I had to get control over something in my life, and controlling my weight, therefore, became my obsession.

I decided that self-induced vomiting was the answer. I started making myself sick when I was sixteen. It never helped me lose weight. Clearly that wasn't what it really was about.

And on top of how I felt about the way I looked, I was sad and lonely in the aftermath of my mother's death. When I looked in the mirror, I saw a fat, motherless kid with pimples who couldn't figure out how to dress or do her hair or do any of the things girls are supposed to know how to do.

But see, the trouble is you start self-inducing vomiting for one reason, or at least you think that's why you're doing it, and it becomes a way to escape the things you're really feeling. By excessively overeating, you become numbed out. Which is a great place to be if you're feeling any of the overwhelming things I was feeling as a teenager. And by physically vomiting, you're expelling more than the ridiculous amounts of food you've ingested. You're expelling whatever you're feeling, whatever you don't understand, all of your difficulties— you're just getting rid of them. I was throwing up the pain of my mother's death, the overwhelming guilt I felt for my role in her sad life, and my sorrow, my mountains of sorrow.

The other thing you're doing, by self-inducing vomiting, is making your body do something it's not supposed to do. And if you are in an exceedingly out-of-control situation, you've mastered control over *some*thing, which gives you a false sense of power.

The bulimia and the drinking didn't have much significance to me then, because I thought everybody was doing it and I assumed I would stop when I wanted to. I was young and thought I was having a good time and could not see into the future. I didn't know that these ways of coping with misery and guilt would follow me for years. Not until I was an adult would I come to deal with them.

Now when I think about my belief that I was overweight, I realize I was actually wrong. After my mother died, my father and Aunt Julia and I took a trip to Maine to look at colleges. When I look at pictures of myself on that trip, I don't see a fat girl. I looked perfectly reasonable. But when I was a small child, I was clearly very chubby. When I was in high school, I *thought* I was fat, but the pictures don't bear that out. Unfortunately, my self-image and my need to use it against myself was already set by high school, and it's been something I've struggled with ever since.

At that point in my life, I wasn't aware in any conscious

way that my sexuality contributed to my sense that I was different. Mostly it felt like whatever was wrong with me was a deficiency of some sort, which was somehow linked to my responsibility for my mother's illness. I rationalized it by thinking that some people are tall, and some people are short. Some people have a romantic life and feel good about how they look, and some people don't. Not until college did I realize I was destined to have a romantic life after all, but it wasn't the kind of romantic life I had planned for.

CHAPTER 5

What I Learned in College

I left home for Trinity College in Hartford, Connecticut, in the fall of 1984. My friends had helped me shop and pack. My father, my friend Dorothy, and I drove up in separate cars. I was excited, of course, and nervous about leaving home.

But leave home I did. I didn't go home on weekends or call home every Sunday. Ellen lived in Connecticut and was only a half hour away, so I had a great safety net and saw her a lot. My dad and I didn't call each other often, but we stayed in close touch in our nontraditional eccentric ways. For example, our primary way of communicating was through his interoffice memo that included a hundred-dollar check. "To: Christine; From: LQ." Or "To: Christine; From: Mr. Quinn." Usually he said nothing else in the memo, but occasionally he'd write, "Attached please find an article I thought you would find of interest." And there'd be a newspaper clipping about Glen Cove or his old neighborhood in the city or something political. That was my father's way, and it still is. You know he's always thinking of you, and his actions speak louder than his words. He wasn't a cuddly father, but he was so endlessly dedicated and attentive and always there when I needed him. He still is.

Just as he had in high school, my father came to every college event he was invited to. He missed only one big occasion when I was at Trinity. It was a parents' weekend, something he loved to attend. But my sophomore year there was a strike at work, and he was a shop steward. He felt bad about missing the weekend, but there was no way he would abandon his responsibilities to travel to Hartford and, besides, he didn't have the money to spend on the weekend. I felt bad that he couldn't make it, but I admired him for his loyalty to his fellow workers.

The fact that my father was the member of a union also made me something of a standout at school. I remember when I'd use my credit card, which was issued by the union, at the college bookstore, they'd take a look at the image on the front of the card—hands locked in a solidarity shake—and look confused or stunned. They weren't being rude about it; they just couldn't process it, because it was out of place for them.

My father called Trinity the preppiest place in America. So when it came to like-minded progressives, there weren't a lot of us. However, the faculty was much more liberal than the students, so I felt I had the support I needed when it came to expressing my political views and doing activism on campus. And because I was an activist working on all kinds of issues and outspoken in general—and probably because of my very loud laugh—I got a reputation for being brash. No doubt I cemented that reputation when I became the Bantam, Trinity's mascot. Here's the story of that.

A bantam is a big fighting rooster, but of course we couldn't have the real thing at Trinity football games. Instead, we had a human inside a bantam costume. It had a big, poufy orange-yellow chest and a head with a beak. The person inside the costume wore orange-gold tights, little yellow feathery shorts, and a blue T-shirt that had a "T" on it. My freshman year I would complain about how awful the Bantam was at the football games. He didn't do much more than walk back and forth and flap his arms. And my friends said, "Stop complaining. You should be the Bantam next year." So I said, "Okay, I'm gonna be the Bantam next year." And I was! I don't think there was much competition for this exalted job, but it was fun. My role as the Bantam was to excite the crowd, torture the cheerleaders by hitting them with their pom-poms, and get the crowd to do chants. And besides, most people didn't know who was underneath the costume, so I had a lot of freedom to be as silly as I wanted.

Then there was the time I got beaten up. Wesleyan was

our rival, and I went over to their side and started running up and down, taunting them. Some guys came down from the stands and started pouring beer all over me, pulling on my beak, and tugging on me. My friend Jon, who was calling the game on the air, sent out an SOS: "This is not a joke! Someone is beating up the Bantam. The Bantam is on the Wesleyan side, and she's getting attacked. Please, people, help." I couldn't get them to stop, so I had to haul around and clock one of the guys. And when I screamed at him, he said, "Oh, I didn't know you were a girl. Sorry." I was all wet and droopy-beaked and had to limp back over to Trinity's side. I went up to the dean of students and said, "Can you believe this? They poured beer on me and were really mean to me." He said, "I hope you had your mouth open," and walked away.

I liked Trinity. There was plenty of social life, and there were lots of different kinds of groups of people. I didn't mind being one of the few liberals on campus—that was totally fine. I hung out with football players, and the jock crowd, and then I hung out with the hippie crowd in the fraternity I joined. I liked bopping around between groups. It was all fun and good, but I was also adrift personally, and because I was never completely rooted in one group it added to that.

I just didn't really care about the classes. They all seemed sort of irrelevant, and they were difficult for me. Until then, school had been a breeze. But college was another thing entirely. I didn't have particularly great study skills, because I'd never had to study that hard before. I am also an unbelievably slow reader, who has to read things a couple of times to digest them. There's a lot of reading in college, and I just couldn't get through it. I had a hard time keeping up. Truth is, I may not have tried that hard, but I bet if you'd asked people, they would've thought I was doing very well in classes. In reality, I was basically just getting by. And then the loss of my mother in the years before college had left me sad and overwhelmed, which made focusing on classes even harder.

I couldn't shrug off the grief and the guilt. They were an enormous distraction, especially when I was supposed to be studying. Even though I knew intellectually, at sixteen, seventeen, eighteen, that I wasn't, I nonetheless felt completely and exclusively responsible for the fact that my mother had gotten sick again and had died. There was little doubt in my mind that it was my fault. I thought that if I had been more attentive to her medications, if I had never shown impatience, or if I had been less demanding, she would have survived. That idea plagued me at college and for many years afterward.

It was part and parcel of my attitude toward myself. On the one hand, I was an energetic leader and a world-class Bantam, but on the other I was not very good at my studies and still overweight. And I was drinking a lot and vomiting a lot. However, I also knew that if I threw myself into an activity, any activity that mattered to me, things would feel a lot better. Maybe I was just keeping with my family tradition. Think of my mother, ill with cancer, putting on theme birthday parties;

or me in high school pulling out all the stops for Sports Night; or my father—despite the burdens of having a sick wife, an elderly mother-in-law, and a sister-in-law living at home— working on the picket line when his men were on strike.

Activity. It was the way of my family, and Trinity was where I discovered my passion for activism. Not that politics was a new interest for me. I was fascinated by it as a kid. I remember wonderful times when I was in my teens, over dinner at my friend's house, when I'd go toe to toe with her father over current events. He was very conservative, and for the most part I managed to hold my own.

I paid close attention when my father talked about his union work and about Democratic politics. His membership in the union guaranteed medical care for our family. If we hadn't had that insurance, my mother's medical expenses might well have bankrupted us.

He gave me two reasons why he was a Democrat. First, he'd say, "Because they met us at the boat." By that he meant the Democrats were there for his family when they came over from Ireland (because the Democrats were—and are— for immigrants). And second, he'd say, "FDR saved my life." He believed deeply that FDR's policies saved his family's lives in the Depression.

I was eager to get involved in such a way that I felt I was having an impact. At the time, there was a big movement on college campuses across the country to get colleges and universities to pull their investments out of South African companies and any companies that did business with South Africa because of that government's apartheid policy. It was an important international movement that helped bring an end to a totally discriminatory government. We got the Trinity student government to pass a resolution urging the college to divest, and a shantytown was set up on campus to represent the shantytowns where South African blacks were restricted to living. Trinity students slept overnight in the shanties. I was so proud to be a part of this effort and felt I was making a difference in some small way.

The best discovery I made at Trinity was that I could do internships through ConnPIRG, an environmental and consumer protection group (founded by Ralph Nader) that watches out for people's interests and "stands up to powerful interests whenever they threaten our health and safety, our financial security or our right to fully participate in our democratic society."

I signed up for every internship and activity I could find and did volunteer work, especially on environmental issues. This work was magical to me. It showed me the amazing strength of people coming together and organizing. It fueled a lifelong belief in the unstoppable power of government and citizens working together. I was assigned to work with a woman who lived a half hour or so from Hartford. Every Saturday we'd knock on doors in her town, surveying residents to document the impact of chemical waste that had been dumped there; it was similar to what had happened in Niagara Falls, New York, where the Love Canal neighborhood was built on top of a toxic waste dump. So we were going door-to-door in her town to try to replicate what had been done at Love Canal, where the government had designated the contaminated area a Superfund site so it could be cleaned up.

Next I lobbied on different pieces of legislation at the statehouse—Trinity is located in Hartford, which is Connecticut's capital. I'd go to the statehouse a day or two every week. I'd grab state representatives in the hallways and talk to them about specific pieces of legislation, like an act to increase funding for household-hazardous-waste-cleanup days, specific days where you could go to a designated site in your community to drop off hazardous waste, like paint thinner and motor oil, that you aren't supposed to put out with your regular garbage. These cleanup days have become a reality in New York City and many other cities and towns. I also worked with the paid lobbyists to help their efforts on specific legislation. And then I'd do the corresponding work on campus to support whatever bill I was lobbying for. That might include getting a petition signed, organizing a letter-writing campaign, or getting students to go up to the statehouse for a lobby day.

During two of my summers at Trinity, I worked to raise money for ConnPIRG. The summer of my sophomore year,

I went door-to-door as a canvasser. I rang bells and asked people to become members of our citizens' network. It was a six-day-a-week job, from ten in the morning until ten or eleven at night. We asked a lot of people to join, but we were intent on helping our cause. The second summer I ran the door-to-door operation, which was easier on my feet but also hard, because the work was exhausting and the turnover was pretty serious.

Going door-to-door is difficult because you're completely intruding on people's lives and space, but it's a great way to get people involved who might not otherwise join. *Wheel of Fortune* was a very popular show that summer, and we were interrupting people in the middle of the show, right when a contestant was about to guess one of the puzzles. So when they opened the door for us, they were already unhappy. That was a challenge. But it's a challenge for every person who puts on a coat and walking shoes and takes to the street to leaflet for something they care about deeply. Nobody likes standing in the rain and interrupting people while they're watching their favorite shows, but this kind of commitment to action is what makes change possible. This work taught me the importance of pushing through the fear of bothering people and asking them to get involved.

During that time I learned how to organize a public event in a way that is most effective and empowering to all in attendance. Room size and the number of chairs are both important. You have to make sure you've got more people saying they'll come to the event than you need to actually show up, because a certain number of people won't show up. And you have to have fewer chairs in the room than the number of people you expect to show up, so the room will look crowded. If more people show up than you expect, then you get more chairs, but you don't want empty seats. You don't want people who've given their precious time feeling like they're the only people who care about something—that will stop them from staying involved!

Doing all this real work on interesting issues was so much better than sitting in a classroom. I was learning how the governmental process worked. It was very hands-on, and I loved it. I was surprised to find that the state representatives were very respectful. They treated me just like anybody else who was there to talk to them about the issues they were working on. This was the best thing for me. I guess I went a bit too far, because not long after I left Trinity, the school imposed a limit on the amount of credit students could get from internships and independent study. You might call that the Chris Quinn rule. I'm fairly sure I was the cause of it, because I'd taken so many internships and probably not enough regular classes.

I wound up majoring in urban studies and education, mostly because I knew that after graduating I wanted to work in politics and government, and these majors made the most sense for me. I'd considered majoring in political science, but everybody in the whole world was a political science major. Besides, when you were a political science major, you had to study national and international issues, and by then my focus was clear: cities fascinated me most—and they still do. I added the education major, not with an eye toward becoming a teacher but to study education from a political perspective.

Once I'd experienced how exciting and satisfying it was to be involved in the political process, I had an even clearer idea of what I wanted to do with my life. As graduation neared, I knew my challenge after Trinity would be to channel my passion for progressive causes, political organizing, and getting things done into some kind of job and profession. I was pretty clueless about how to make that happen in a self-sustaining way, but I was determined to find a way.

A more complicated challenge waited in the background.

While I had a very busy social life at Trinity and enjoyed spending time with my friends, my romantic life was just as nonexistent as it had been in high school. Not that there was a lot of pressure to date at Trinity—there wasn't. Every college has a different social dynamic. I didn't know anyone at Trinity who went out on dates, and compared with other schools, there weren't even that many couples. One of my high school classmates went to a college in the South, where if you didn't have a date you didn't go to football games. Trinity was nothing like that. So I never really felt left out.

Then again, I just assumed I was *always* going to be left out, which is different from feeling left out. I had no expectation that I'd ever get asked out on a date and had no interest either, so it's not like I was disappointed. It was what it was. Then, during my senior year and much to my dismay, I discovered that I wasn't immune to romantic feelings.

To this day, I vividly remember my first crush, although the funny thing is, I can't remember her name. I just remember her big halo of curly hair. We were both seniors, but she was probably in her midtwenties because she'd taken time off to travel. I'd see her in some of my classes, and on occasion we talked. We were friendly but not supergood friends, and I certainly never told her about my feelings for her.

Normally a crush is kind of a fluttery feeling. You feel excited and anxious, but not in a bad way. And when you're in that state of mind, your friends will tell you it's a crush. It's a universal experience that's celebrated in music and poetry. But to me, all those fluttery feelings were overshadowed by a troubling sensation, because I was having them for a girl. And so those feelings were wrong.

Looking back, it's hard to say exactly how I knew my feelings were wrong. I don't remember hearing any sermons in church about it. It didn't come up once in religion or theology classes. I don't remember being taught about it in school at all. And my parents never indicated one way or the other how they felt about LGBT people. But I saw and heard things that probably had a subconscious impact on what I thought about being gay. When I was a child, other kids did use the word *gay* in a negative way. I don't think those young kids were aware of being homophobic—I'm not even sure they knew what *gay* meant.

In sixth or seventh grade, I got called *dyke* by kids at school. Again, I don't know how I knew what that word meant, because I have no memory of ever having heard it before, but I must have because I knew it was bad and knew enough to say, "No, no, I have a crush on" a certain boy. Of course I didn't have a crush on any boy and never really have, but I said it to prove that I wasn't what they said I was. I didn't say a word to my parents or to my sister about the episode because I was afraid. I must have wanted to tell them, because I must have been frightened and upset—at least enough that the experience remains vivid to this day.

I grew up in a homophobic era. You didn't have to hear a sermon about it or know what your parents thought about it. It was in the air. At least it was in Glen Cove in the 1970s. What I saw at college was better, but far from perfect. Trinity wasn't exactly on the cutting edge of college LGBT rights activism. By the mid-1960s and early 1970s, Columbia and Vassar had out students and gay student organizations. But in 1984, when I was a freshman, a senior came out in a letter to the editor in the school newspaper. (I'm not sure if he was the first out gay student at Trinity, but he was the first to come out in such a public way.)

I happened to know him because I volunteered for a community outreach program that he'd founded. Trinity is situated in a very poor neighborhood, at the top of an enormous hill. When you're on campus, you literally overlook the poor neighborhood below. There was quite a lot of tension between the students, who were largely affluent, and the people who lived in the surrounding neighborhood. So this guy was already known on campus for his great community work, and his coming out was something people talked about, which I imagine was what he'd hoped people would do.

Trinity already had an LGBT student organization by the time I got there, and while they didn't publicize their meetings (because they'd had problems with other students throwing things at members as they came and went), a group of them would routinely visit classes. They'd ask professors to give them a block of class time so they could talk about homophobia and LGBT issues, and then they'd answer questions. During the years I was there, they came to a few of my classes, and I thought they were so very brave, articulate, and well put together. Sometimes people would ask stupid questions, but given how little people knew back then, I'm guessing they were just trying to understand something that made them uncomfortable—or they were just knuckleheaded. After four years at Trinity, I had a full, positive political awareness about LGBT people and the LGBT civil rights movement. I thought discrimination was wrong, and I was fully supportive of efforts to pass antidiscrimination legislation. But I was not gay.

I had that crush on the senior with curly hair, but when I tried to picture myself leading a gay life, I couldn't. It was all uncharted territory. Actually, a lot of my life had *already* felt like uncharted territory. To paraphrase something my father often says, I needed uncharted territory like a moose needs a hat rack. So I decided to push my feelings aside. I went back to my tiny dorm room, closed the door, sat on my bed, and talked to myself and to God. I said out loud, "This is not going to happen to you." It wasn't so much that I pretended I didn't have the feelings I was having. I just pushed them down so deep that they no longer existed, because being interested in women—being a lesbian—was not the plan, at least not the plan for me.

That seems like a lifetime ago, and in many ways it was. I'm now very comfortable living as openly as I do—my wedding photo was on the front page of the *New York Times*! But when I'm really honest with myself, I have to admit that, like so many LGBT people, in the back of my mind I still have a faint sense of unease, wondering what people will think of me when I walk into unfamiliar situations, fearing they will judge me because of who I am. I suppose that given the times I grew up in, it's understandable that even an out and proud lesbian like me still looks over her shoulder when no one is watching.

The world has changed, and I hope I've contributed just a little bit to that change. As I left the embracing arms of the Trinity campus with the lessons I had learned, about my identity and about social change, I embarked on a new chapter and entered into real life.

Part II

Learning My City, Finding Myself

CHAPTER 6

Winning and Losing

I wasn't sure how I was going to get there, but my life's work already had a direction. It came from two sources, I think. The influence of my parents is in my bones. My father's union activism showed me that when people stick together, great things can happen and people's lives are improved. My mother was often sick and very tired, but her illness and her pain gave her momentum. She was going to make things better for people and me whenever or however she could. And she knew she didn't have forever to do it, so she didn't waste a minute. Years later Ellen told me that all those afternoons in the car, when my mother drove me from lesson to lesson, had one overriding purpose in her mind: to raise me well and see me through grammar school. That was her stated goal. She lived a few years longer, but her imprint has lasted all my life.

The other big factors are my personality and my internal makeup. I really like being with people and doing things with them, and it has always made me feel good to get things done. Perhaps it started when I was a kid. It was often lonely in the house, and so whenever I could, I would run outside to be with my gang of friends. I needed them, and the best way to do things with them was to organize them. It wasn't for nothing that they called me the Mayor of Libby Drive. I have carried this passion with me ever since: whenever I see a problem, I want to fix it. Maybe the fact that I couldn't fix my mother, that I couldn't stop her inevitable decline from the cancer, drives me. I don't want to go overboard here, but I'm happiest in a group, and I like the fun of making things happen. Another well-known aspect of my personality is that I can be loud. Can it have come from living with two almost-deaf relatives, my mother and Aunt Julia? And my laugh is the loudest! I love a good story or a great joke.

This is a decent set of character traits for someone who wants to make social change her life's goal. After Trinity, I struggled to find the right job. I was offered a six-month stint in Boston as a field organizer for an antinuclear referendum, which sought to close down the two nuclear power plants in Massachusetts. It was a PIRG-affiliated effort.

I was responsible for organizing house parties to get people to support our effort and vote in favor of the referendum. We did a lot of door-to-door canvassing. Before we went out, we'd practice by doing role-playing. You would pretend to knock on a door. Someone pretending to be a resident would come to the door, and you'd recite your script to them. That person would respond to what you said, and you'd pivot into whatever the right response was. The PIRG really drilled into our heads the significance of practicing, and anyone on my staff now can tell you—I believe in practicing.

We held some public events. Once again I learned that you don't want to organize an event in a room that's too big for the number of people you're expecting; otherwise it will look empty, and that's demoralizing to the people who do show up. If they've left their homes to go out to an event they think is important, and nobody else is there, it makes them think that what they care about doesn't matter. That's depressing, and you run the risk of having those people never come out again, or they wind up having a negative feeling about public citizenship, which is just the opposite of what you're trying to instill.

I also learned that you never hold a meeting unless you have an "ask" for the people in the room. Once you get people there, you'd better be prepared to ask them to do something: sign a petition, donate their time or money, or agree to do volunteer work. If you don't ask for something, they won't feel like they're involved. After all, if people have bothered to come to the meeting in the first place, it's because they care about the issue you're promoting. So you waste a huge opportunity if you don't ask them to do something that will contribute to whatever you're campaigning for.

The other big lesson I learned from that referendum campaign was about the importance of follow-up. I became the queen of follow-up. You have to get back to people with what they've asked for, whether it's basic information, or a way for them to get involved, or whatever. The key is responding. You can't leave people hanging, because then they get discouraged and won't come back the next time you ask for help with a referendum or an election or any kind of community effort.

We were trying to get the citizens of Massachusetts to vote to close down two nuclear power plants, but public opinion was not in our favor. And neither were the most important Massachusetts political leaders. We worked hard, and we did our best, but we lost miserably. That was a lesson for me. Can you imagine? Our debrief on the campaign was about how much *damage* we'd done to the antinuclear movement! I was too young and inexperienced to have seen it coming, but however disappointing it was to lose, it was still a good organizing experience. Winning probably hadn't been in the cards, but winning is only one way things can go.

Sadly, when I got back home, Aunt Julia was in the last stages of colon cancer. She was a difficult patient. Her deafness made it hard for her to grasp what we were telling her and what was happening to her. Also, she was in a powerful state of denial, convinced that if she prayed enough, God would intervene and save her. I had already buried my mother from cancer, and the idea that God would intervene—or had ever intervened—in her life to make everything right made me nuts. This wasn't about faith. It was about cancer. In the best of times, Julia had always had trouble adapting, and these were far from the best of times. As her health declined, she became more and more withdrawn, frightened, and therefore uncooperative.

We had to be tough with her, and that was not fun. One time the home health aide asked for my help because Aunt Julia couldn't get out of the bathtub and had become somewhat hysterical. It was hard to get through to her that she had to let one of us help her out of the tub, so I said very firmly, "Look, you let me pick you up, or I'm calling the police department to come and do it." That caught her attention—she knew me well enough to know that I'd call the police if I had to. She didn't want the police coming in and seeing her naked, so she let me pick her up. Julia died on March 4, 1989, and we had the funeral at the same funeral home and church where we'd had my mother's funeral. Four years later, almost to the day, we would hold my grandmother Nellie's funeral there, too.

Grief sometimes drags you down, and the situation in Glen Cove was sad; but it also left me with a sense of the limited time we have, and that propelled me forward. So I began my job search for work as a political organizer. It's hard for me to imagine it, but I didn't have even one connection in New York City politics or know a single person who had any. I needed a job, so I became an administrative assistant at the Friends of Channel 13, a group of affluent women who raised money for public television. I told myself that at least I had a do-good job that offered a paycheck.

I moved to the city, into an apartment with a friend from high school whose mother would only let her live on the Upper East Side. We lived on East Eighty-ninth between First and York. There was a certain irony to that address. My father had grown up just a few blocks north, at Ninety-sixth and First. He had loved the neighborhood. In his day it was not really such a great place at all, but in his eyes it was absolutely heaven. My grandfather also was enormously fond of Yorkville and its wonderful immigrant community. Even though he drove a bus, he longed to own profitable real estate. But he felt that the real estate potential of Ninety-sixth and First Avenue was lacking. It was a two-fare zone on mass transit, and so he thought it would never become nice. A bus driver sees the city from behind the wheel of the bus. That was his perspective. Every New Yorker has a personal view of this city.

I knew that Channel 13 wasn't for me in the long run, so I searched for another job when my boss was out of the office. I really wanted to do political organizing around the issues I cared about like housing, education, health care, and the environment. I made telephone calls to people whose names I saw in the papers, and I'd ask them to have coffee or lunch with me. I'd learned to do that when I was organizing in college. If I was organizing an event, I'd read the weekly newspapers and highlight the names of the important people in the town who were mentioned in the stories. I'd make a list of those people and call them.

Cold-calling people produces a lot of anxiety if you let yourself think about it. So I tried not to think about it. You have to treat it like ripping off a Band-Aid or going off a diving board. I learned that if you call people and ask them for help, even people you don't know, they are often remarkably interested in assisting you. People actually perceive getting a request for help as a big compliment. It means the caller sees something in them. And every successful person has been helped along the way, so many of them are happy to pay back by helping a newcomer.

A funny thing happened with my calls. Early on in my job search, a lot of people would call back because they thought I was Chris *Glen,* who was a high-profile judge at the time. (She was later dean of the CUNY Law School.) Occasionally people would say, "Hi, Your Honor!" and I'd have to tell them I wasn't Chris Glen, but they generally stayed on the phone anyway and talked to me and advised me. I got all kinds of suggestions and leads that way and eventually found a job as a housing organizer at the Association for Neighborhood Housing and Development (ANHD). I didn't know it then, but the job would set me on the path to a life of public service. ANHD is a group I still work with today as Speaker.

In my new position, I ran the Housing Justice Campaign. It was a great job, because ANHD is a network of housing groups all across the city. I got to advocate on their behalf— from the end of the Ed Koch administration into the David Dinkins administration, and before the City Council— lobbying for funds in the budget (which is kind of ironic, given the job I have now). For example, Mayor Koch had a ten-year plan to build tens of thousands of affordable housing units across the city. We worked on trying to make that plan even bigger and better. We tried to reverse cuts in the city budget that affected housing, and we worked to eliminate or reform programs that we thought were a waste of money. My work also focused on getting funding for the community-based housing groups we represented.

To do all this, I got to meet with the different groups. I visited all kinds of neighborhoods around the city where I'd never been before. I met amazing people who were developing campaigns and programs on housing issues and fighting for tenants. I got to know people I would never have met, and they were great.

They had awesome stories about their neighborhoods.

On the Lower East Side, for example, somebody had heard a rumor that something was going down at City Hall, at the Board of Estimate, at nine o'clock that night. So people ran around the neighborhood to the six different coffee shops and bars and barbershops where their friends hung out, and they all literally ran to City Hall. Whatever it was that had been slipped on the government's agenda for that meeting, they stopped. For me, the idea that people would know exactly who was at which bar and which diner was thrilling. It was beyond exciting that a neighborhood's sense of itself was so complete that people knew where everybody else was and how to find them.

I went to the South Bronx and to Williamsburg and to Hell's Kitchen. Everywhere I went, I met a different group. It was fascinating—from Banana Kelly in the South Bronx to St. Nick's in Greenpoint, everybody was doing ostensibly the same thing, but with its own flavor, depending on the makeup of the neighborhood and its needs. At St. Nick's in Greenpoint the neighborhood was then very, very Polish, so they had to have Polish-speaking staff. Banana Kelly, in the late 1980s, was still trying to figure out how to work with the city-owned property that existed but needed to be rebuilt from top to bottom. That was different from Williamsburg, which was more built; the group there was dealing with land-lord issues. I found out that you can't stick with one model of anything in this city—the problems, the needs, and the solutions change from neighborhood to neighborhood.

These places were and are remarkable. Every neighborhood has its own people, its own special places, and its own identity. Today it's getting harder and harder for neighborhoods, but they still exist, and there are always new pockets of people, and new diners or coffee shops or other places where community is built. These little pockets of people are full of personality and identity and energy. The conversations, the gossip, the moving from place to place, and the stories make Facebook and other social media look like virtual copies of the real thing. It was fun, and the people were funny. I liked to sit and listen to their stories. I still do.

As I explored the city's different neighborhoods and met with the various community housing groups and community leaders, I found a city that was so much more diverse than I'd ever imagined. And the issues concerning housing were much more complicated than I'd expected. But I was also impressed by how many people were trying to fix the problems. It was exhilarating to have the opportunity to work with community groups and elected officials citywide on an important issue that carried the possibility of helping to improve people's lives.

I learned a lot, too, about how the City Council works, how the budget process works, and how city government in general works. In my interactions with public officials, I discovered that based on the years of dealing with my mother, I could read the body language of people and then I could figure things out on my feet. I could think while I was in motion. Maybe I inherited that ability from my grandmother Nellie Callaghan, who knew you could pray while running.

This job had other life-changing impacts. For one, I met Tom Duane at an ANHD-related event concerning tenants. Neither of us can remember which event it was, so in recent years whenever Tom and I are at a tenant or housing rally, we'll joke and say, "*This* is the issue we met over!" Tom was working for the City Comptroller's office, but he was mostly biding his time to try a second run for City Council. He lost in 1989, but with an upcoming expansion of the City Council from thirty-five to fifty-one members, Tom stood a good chance of winning in a district—the West Village, Chelsea, and Hell's Kitchen—that was likely to elect an openly gay candidate.

I liked Tom from the first. He was funny and outgoing and interesting. He had this teddy-bear quality that made him very appealing. And he was a big deal. In his first run for City Council, he almost took out a longtime incumbent. This meeting eventually led to my joining Tom's campaign in the winter of 1990 as a volunteer working evenings and weekends. I was involved in a lot of planning and strategy and fund-raising meetings. I also met Tom's team of advisers and volunteers.

The following May I took a leave of absence from ANHD to become part of his paid staff, as the campaign manager. For the next four months, it was 24/7. I had to raise money, figure out the strategy, develop the direct mail pieces, recruit and manage the volunteers, get the phone script ready so the volunteers could call potential voters, identify potential voters, find a press person, create a press plan, read the mail, and respond to whatever the crisis of the day was.

As in any political campaign, I had to keep a zillion balls in the air at once, and whatever I thought was going to happen on one day was almost never what did happen that day. The most important things were to keep things moving and to manage the candidate so that he could execute the campaign plan. We had a paid staff of four and a lot of volunteers. It was hard work and a lot of it. And if I had not been struggling with feelings that I couldn't keep at bay any longer, it would have been the best year of my life.

As soon as I officially joined Tom's campaign staff, he introduced me to everyone as his "straight campaign manager." He was so excited that he had a straight manager, as only Tom could be. I think he got a kick out of it because no one would have expected him to have one. The problem was, I wasn't straight, and it was getting more and more difficult for me to keep up the pretense—even to myself—that I was straight.

I was in denial about my sexuality. Let's face it. I had enough on my plate, I thought. As a teenager I had decided that I would never have a personal life, and that was a great way to put my real feelings into a box and bury them. But as I was finding myself in my work, which I loved, I could no longer hide from who I was.

Enter Laura, who had been Tom's campaign volunteer coordinator on his first campaign. She came back to volunteer in 1991 and was part of his strong kitchen cabinet, so she was around all the time. She was an out lesbian. She was very involved in ACT UP and Queer Nation. Being LGBT wasn't the problem for Laura that it still was for me. It soon became clear that she was interested in me. She was sweet with me. She would hang around and be attentive, while I was uncomfortable and awkward.

Quite frankly, I was clueless about flirting and dating. I would have been just as flummoxed if it had been a guy flirting with me. No one—male or female—had ever expressed that kind of interest in me before, so I was totally inexperienced. Funny—my inexperience didn't keep me from flirting back. It seemed to come naturally, and somehow I forgot that I had promised never to let this kind of thing happen.

When I realized where things were headed, I decided I had to call a halt to it. One night when Laura and I were working late at the campaign office, I said, "Look, I'm flattered that you've been flirting with me and I know I've been flirting back, but I shouldn't have done it. I'm sorry that I did and I'm going to stop it because this can't happen. I'm not going to be gay." It didn't occur to me that Laura would be upset on both a personal and political level. Personally, because I was telling her that despite my flirting nothing was going to happen; and politically, because to say I wasn't going to be gay when I was gay was unacceptable to her as an activist. I was still in a frame of mind where I just wasn't going to let this happen. Being LGBT was not going to work for me. Life was challenging enough, so why take on something that would make it even tougher? I didn't need another challenge.

It makes me cringe to think of this exchange and of what I said. But I felt the same kind of self-loathing that so many men and women feel. I'm just lucky that Laura had the smarts and patience to stick with me. The next morning I called her to see if she was okay. She said, "How do you think I am? I'm terrible!" She came to the campaign office that evening, and when we finished up, I had to take some packages to the post office, so we went together and talked afterward. I explained what I'd been thinking the night before but hadn't been able to articulate, about how I didn't want this to happen and why. She listened and was very understanding. I guess that's what I needed. Things went from me saying that it wasn't going to happen to *it* happening. Laura and I lived together for the next seven years.

So now I had another river to cross. I was no longer the straight campaign manager for the first openly gay candidate for City Council. I had to tell Tom that Laura and I were seeing each

other. It strikes me as idiotic that I was worried about coming
out to my boss, an extremely up-front LGBT leader in New
York City. But I was scared. I had never done this before.

So I chose my moment carefully—or maybe not. We
were on the subway heading downtown to a Rent Guidelines
Board hearing, where Tom was scheduled to testify. While
sitting on the train at the City Hall subway station, I said,
"Tom, I have something serious to tell you."

He panicked. "Oh my God, you're going to quit!"

I shook my head.

"Oh my God, you're a lesbian!"

I nodded and told him I was seeing Laura. Then we discussed his testimony for the hearing. Later, as we were walking into the auditorium where the hearing was taking place,
I said, "Tom, we really need to talk about this." And he said,
"Yeah, we'll find time," which we did at breakfast the next
morning after we'd been out distributing leaflets.

Tom told me he was happy for me and would be there
for me if I ever wanted to talk. He made it clear that it was
no big deal. And then it was back to the campaign, because
there was just too much to do and nothing much more to
say. My big drama didn't disturb the people in the office—
they wanted me to be happy. I appreciated their support
and warmth, especially as I began to consider how to break
the news to my father. I fretted over it for months. Finally, I
knew I had to get it over with, so I called him and told him I
wanted to come see him after work.

We saw each other a lot, but a visit out of nowhere must have seemed a little unusual. After Aunt Julia died, he got out of Glen Cove quickly. He'd sold our house and moved to a one-bedroom apartment on the Upper West Side of Manhattan. But he brought way too much furniture with him—almost everything from the living room and family room—and jammed it all into his apartment. So there were lots of places to sit, but there wasn't a lot of room to move around. He brought fourteen chairs, which I know because I counted them as they came off the moving van.

I was in a hurry to get this over with, so as soon as I arrived, we sat down in the living room across from each other. He was on the blue sofa, and I was in one of the club chairs. I was feeling anxious and fearful, because as much as I hoped it would go well, I knew it could go terribly wrong. I had heard all kinds of stories about people coming out, ranging from Hallmark moments, which this most likely wasn't going to be, to horrible situations where the family never spoke to the person again, which I didn't expect either.

It helped that my sister already knew. Unfortunately, she had found out in a way that was awkward and hurtful, and I still feel bad about it. She had been trying for weeks to reach me at my apartment in Brooklyn, but I was spending most of my time at Laura's apartment. After calling a bunch of times and not getting a callback from me, she finally badgered my old roommate into giving her Laura's phone number. Laura was one of the people who ran the Gay and Lesbian Independent Democrats, so her answering machine said: "You can leave a message here for Gay and Lesbian Independent Democrats or Laura."

It wasn't much of a leap for Ellen to figure things out, and when she did, she was angry. Not at the truth, mind you, but at me, for not telling her myself. She was totally right—I should have. But I was afraid, and it's not like I had much of a family by this time. My mother and aunt and grandparents were gone, so it was just me, my sister, and my father.

I hadn't lost Ellen at all, but now here I was risking my relationship with my father, at a time when I was still on shaky ground. I hoped I was doing the right thing. There's that moment before you take a leap into the unknown, which I was about to do with my father, when you have to remind yourself to breathe so you can take the next step. I took a deep breath.

"I have something to tell you," I said. "I wanted to let you know that I'm in a relationship with Laura, and I'm gay."

Without hesitating and with an edge in his voice, my father said, "Never say that again."

His words were disappointing, but not surprising, and they stung. I struggled not to get angry in response. Instead I said, "Well, okay, but I'm going to say it again to whomever I want to say it to. I've lived up to my responsibility by telling you, so what you do with the information is up to you."

He said, "Let's go get dinner."

We walked over to the Popover Café. We weren't there very long, but with nothing to talk about other than what we'd read in the newspaper that day, it felt like an eternity. It was incredibly awkward. Clearly he wanted to get out of there and go home. And honestly, so did I. It was a relief to have told him the truth about my life, and I took comfort in knowing I'd done the right thing, but I was hurt. And now I was in the land of uncertainty because I had no way of knowing how things with my father would be. I hoped eventually he'd come around.

And he has, in remarkable, almost unimaginable ways. Not exactly in words, but in presence and deeds.

I've had a lot of time to think about what happened in my father's apartment that night and why he reacted as he did. I'm pretty sure he knew I was gay by then, but he lived in a world where people didn't feel the need to talk about things, even if they were obvious. It was awkward enough for him that the thing I was telling him about was outside his realm of experience, but the fact that I felt the need to tell him in the first place was well beyond his realm.

My father is an honest and loving man, blessed with a wry sense of humor. But my confession put him on the spot and rendered him speechless. It didn't feel good when it happened, and it hasn't always been easy since then. Sometimes he would distance himself, and sometimes I'd do the same. Then I'd ask Ellen to intervene. Daddy is a little afraid of Ellen—and so am I. We both pretty much do what she says.

My father and I have a unique and significant way of communicating, and in reality we are extremely close, although ours is different from many father-daughter relationships. We both know how much love there is between us, and even if we don't express it in words, we show it in actions. It helps to remember—and I have to remind myself—that my father exists on two planes that are contradictory, which I think a lot of parents of gay children face, especially those whose religious tenets conflict with their love for their child.

But the most important thing about my father is that he reached beyond a lifetime of traditional beliefs in order to support and embrace me, my friends—who have become *his* friends—my work, and the woman I love. He is there whenever he is needed—he's introduced me at every State of the City address I've given since I was elected Speaker in 2006. He marches every year in New York City's LGBT pride parade. And he walked me down the aisle at my wedding.

My dad has spent a ton of time stuffing envelopes for LGBT efforts and going to LGBT events. He still makes jokes. He calls the Gay and Lesbian Independent Democrats the "Gaelic League of Independent Democrats." And he told my sister that doing mailings for all these different LGBT groups was the twentieth-century version of a gay quilting bee—you all sit around a table, stuff envelopes, and talk.

It took time for my father to reach this point. I can't say I know what the journey has been like for him. As I've said, we're not a family that talks about such things. But for me the most significant lesson is that people have an enormous ability to evolve and accept. You can't demand that everyone evolve and accept in the ways you want them to, but things work out. And the love that exists between my father and me is palpable. Though it is silent in words, it is loud in deeds.

CHAPTER 7

Duane's World

When I first went to work for Tom Duane's 1991 campaign, we didn't know who his opponent in the primary would be. It was a newly redrawn district that was heavily LGBT. The incumbent decided not to run again, and then Liz Abzug, whose mother was the legendary feminist liberal congresswoman Bella Abzug, decided to run. Liz was also LGBT.

· Tom had very deep roots as a neighborhood and LGBT activist. As my father used to say, "The man joined everything!" He had been a district leader and a community board member, and he had written a zoning plan for the neighborhood, for starters. It was almost impossible to identify a local issue that Tom hadn't been involved in, at least tangentially.

He was committed to the people in his district on all levels, and he felt a personal urgency around LGBT issues and HIV and AIDS.

Tom was HIV positive. He told me this in a completely roundabout way one night, and we often still joke about it.

He called me late one evening at work when I was the only person in the office, and he said, "They formed this new HIV-positive Democratic club, and they're going to have their first meeting."

"Great, you should go," I said.

"Well, it's only for people who are HIV positive," he said. "It's not for allies."

"Well, I think you can probably still go as a candidate," I said.

And he said, "Well, I *am* HIV positive, so if I go more people will know."

Only a bit surprised, I shook my head. *How are we going to deal with this?* I wondered. But Tom knew—he already had a plan.

Tom had to be honest about his HIV status, and he was determined to be, so there was never any question that he would go public. But we had no idea how people would react. And we could not anticipate the potential fallout. Today it would not be as major an issue, but you have to put yourself back into history. This was 1991. AIDS was still a complete epidemic.

There was real prejudice against people who were infected with HIV and tremendous fear about the disease. As far as we could tell, Tom would be the first openly HIV-positive person to run for public office anywhere in the world. We lacked precedents for what was happening, but luckily a volunteer on the campaign was a public relations director for a large nonprofit, and he helped us develop a plan and manage the media storm.

We settled on sending out, at the beginning of the campaign, a very simple personal letter from Tom to all his constituents, in which he discussed his HIV status. We leaked a copy of the letter to the *New York Times* and timed the mailing so that the letter would get to people the same day the *Times* story broke. So that morning there was a cover story in the *Times*'s Metro section about Tom's HIV status. (Back then there was still a separate Metro section with local news.)

We had arranged for Tom to be out leafleting at a subway entrance on the corner of Eighth Avenue and Twenty-third Street that morning. The response was beyond anything anyone could have imagined. Dozens of reporters and photographers and television cameras showed up at a press conference later that day, and Tom calmly took everyone's questions. The night before the *Times* story, the phone rang off the hook, and the PR guy who was helping us said, "Just don't answer it." Those were the days of answering machines, and we could hear all the messages people were leaving. One of the calls was from the *New York Post,* which had gotten wind of the letter we had leaked to the *Times.* I'll never forget this one message, in a voice that was classic New Yawkese: "Will somebody pleeeeease cawwwwwwl the *Neeeeeew Yaaaaawk Post!*"

Tom's campaign team was a typical Duane mix: old-time neighborhood campaign people, LGBT folks, people who had been engaged in politics for a couple of races, and gay folks who were newer to the political scene. AIDS and LGBT activists seized the opportunity to help elect the first openly gay and openly HIV-positive candidate for City Council.

And you have to add my father to the mix, because when I went to work for Tom—as in everything else I have done—he came along with me. My father likes to joke that he virtually financed Tom's campaign. That's an exaggeration, but he was certainly generous and involved. If you ask him, he'll tell you that he bought eight dollars' worth of bagels for the campaign staffers and volunteers every day, which they really appreciated. He drove volunteers to places where they set up tables for campaigning. People loved him. He's funny and colorful and entertaining. And he enjoyed it, too, and I loved having him around.

My dad is a terrific storyteller. And he sure has stories, from both past and present. His Irish roots and working-class history make for quite an epic. And his years as shop steward at Sperry are the source of a tale or two. Telling stories, and telling them well, is an art. And my father is a master. He is also a very good active listener. So the people I worked with then, and the people I work with now, came to admire him and enjoy spending time with him. He's quirky and funny, and he's always there in a great way.

The thing I quickly discovered about running a campaign was that you have absolutely no time to manage things in an orderly way—it's so fast moving. You don't have the luxury of sitting down with someone to talk. I learned to be grateful and appreciative when I could tell people what they were doing well, because undoubtedly I'd have to point out what they were doing wrong, too. A campaign is not always a matter of management, but it is always a matter of momentum.

Tom and I complemented each other's strengths and weaknesses most of the time. We are both stubborn and have tempers, and during the campaign—and later when I was his chief of staff—we'd sometimes get into it. When I feel like I'm not being listened to, like I'm being disregarded, it gets to me. I try to control my temper, but sometimes I can't help it, and with Tom things could get pretty heated. Whenever that happened, after the storm passed Tom would reassure the staff that everything was okay by saying something like "Mommies and daddies often fight, but it doesn't mean they don't love each other." We were an unusual set of parents—and we loved each other.

In New York City, the primary happens in September and the election follows in November. We knew Tom would have no significant challenger in November, so the primary was the real election for us. Primary day was a huge managerial operation. You sent people out to leaflet at the subways and the polling places, to put up posters, to knock on doors, and to make sure the phone banks were running, that kind of stuff. You'd break up the district into sectors, and the sector coordinators would drive around in cars checking in on the different polling places to make sure the people you had assigned to be at the polls had enough leaflets and other supplies. The people assigned to the polls had to call in to campaign headquarters in the morning, at midday, and at five p.m. to give us the number of people who had voted. We'd get calls about this or that machine not working, and we had to deal with any other problems that came up.

I stayed in our storefront office on Eighth Avenue all day coordinating things. By evening, it was pretty clear Tom was going to win. Everybody was gathering at the restaurant next door: volunteers, supporters, press, and elected officials. It was packed. At some point Tom arrived and was surrounded by a sea of people. I watched from the back of the room.

On election night you're on adrenaline, so you're thrilled and exhausted and exhilarated all at the same time. It was an incredible high, especially because I knew how much Tom's win meant to so many people whose voices hadn't been heard in city government before. His election was a turning point. This was the third or fourth time a gay person had run for that particular City Council seat, but it was the first time a gay person had won. After all this effort and all this time, it felt like a ceiling had cracked. The community had battled the government for recognition and for the gay rights bill, and were still fighting for better funding for HIV and AIDS. They had waged so many battles, and they would fight many more, but this was a great victory. We had no illusions that the trials were over, but now at least we'd have somebody on the inside helping the fight. And as Tom's new chief of staff, I'd have a chance to help with all these efforts.

Chief of staff to a City Council member" may sound like a big title, but in truth I was the chief cook and bottle washer. The offices for councilmembers were, and still are, not big. We had a staff of three or four. My job was to manage the staff, oversee the legislative and budget work, coordinate the press and the scheduler, and oversee the staff's work with constituents and the local community boards.

New York City has a total of fifty-nine community boards with about fifty members each. Community boards have an advisory role on everything from transportation to zoning. In our district, we basically had three community boards (and small pieces of two others—community board and City Council districts don't cover exactly the same territory), and we were expected to have staff people at all their meetings. There are a lot of community board and other community meetings, and if we failed to send somebody to a meeting, it would not go unnoticed.

My father, who often volunteered to answer the phone at our district office, tells the story of a community board member who called to complain. They'd had a subcommittee meeting of some kind the night before, and the board member said, "Duane's office wasn't there."

"No, you're mistaken, I know we were there," my father said.

"I have the attendance list right here in front of me, and you *weren't!*" the caller replied. It was *that* kind of district, so you did your best to make sure you had a staffer at every meeting and every place they needed to be. People really care, and they demand and should get attention. That's what makes our city great.

A flood of letters came in from constituents, and to deal with them, I developed a system to make sure that nothing slipped through the cracks. In those days, constituent complaints and requests came by regular mail, and there were thousands of them. A staff member would photocopy the front cover of every piece of mail that got forwarded to them, and that copy would go into its own folder for the staff person to deal with. We'd meet once a week to go through the folders. If the constituent's problem had been addressed, we'd take the copy out of the folder and close the case. If there were still issues, we'd write ways to deal with the problem on the copy. The designated staff person would follow up that week. The next week we'd go through the folders again, so that ultimately everything would be addressed in some way or another.

I've always said to staff who work with constituents that even if you don't have an immediate answer, it's better to call that person back or write to them and say, for example, "I'm waiting to hear from the Department of Buildings, and I share your frustration over the delay." Because what the constituent wants, besides an answer to his or her question, is to know that they're being heard.

I believe it's essential to respond to every letter, e-mail, and phone call that comes in from constituents, and to do so in a timely way. The person who takes time out of a busy day to write a letter to their elected official deserves to have it recognized and to know that the people who work for them are paying attention to them. Your constituents are your customers, your clients, and the people you work for. It's their government, and they're paying for it. If you don't respond, you wind up forever coloring a citizen's opinion of government in a negative way. This management technique turns up in successful customer-oriented businesses, but back then we were devising seat-of-the-pants solutions to problems that mattered to us.

For Tom, constituent work came naturally, but he faced the same kind of challenge that almost every new councilmember faces: figuring out how to go from who you were before you were elected—usually some type of neighborhood activist—to this new position, where you not only have to represent your district and your local constituency but you are also expected to weigh in on broader, citywide issues. Tom was particularly interested in neighborhood preservation and land use. And because he was the first openly gay and openly HIV-positive councilmember, he was very interested in promoting domestic partnership legislation. He was the strongest voice in the council for issues concerning HIV and AIDS. He felt a particular responsibility to represent all New Yorkers affected by HIV and AIDS and who were LGBT, because he could do it with the kind of authority and passion that no one else on the council could.

Like all elected official's offices, we needed to build support for Tom's work by getting press, and here my high school and college experiences came in handy. Our great mix of people and our funny and flexible councilmember came up with all kinds of ways to get people to pay attention to our issues. Some were great and impossible, and some were worth a try. For example, for a health-care press conference on the issue of getting growth hormones out of milk, we had someone dress up like a cow and stand on the steps of City Hall.

Another time we went after landlords who were failing to take care of their buildings or harassing their tenants to get them to move out so they could raise their rents. We had a slogan, "Landlords are skunks, they make our neighbor-hood stink," which was accurate, if a bit harsh, and it got people's attention. For that press conference and picket, we had someone dress up like a skunk. Then there was the (not so)famous turkey episode. Later, when I was on the council, we found out that the old McBurney YMCA, which used to be on Twenty-third Street, was selling its building and was going to evict its tenants from the SRO. It was all going to happen around Thanksgiving. So we had our intern dress up in a turkey costume to get attention for our protest.

I was always renting costumes. Was this a holdover from my Sports Nights and from my year as Trinity's Bantam mascot? Or was it just fun? It was all of the above, and it was good for getting press attention. We learned from other elected officials that if you did a press conference on a Sunday, which is often a slow news day, and you had someone dressed in a costume to illustrate an important campaign issue, you'd usually get press.

Daily life in a City Council office was generally driven by what was on the calendar: hearings, budget meetings, and community board meetings. If tenants in the district were having a problem with their landlord, you might see whether there was a legislative solution to their issue. In general, for a new councilmember, it's very hard to get any kind of leg-islation passed because you don't have seniority. Our activist experience made us also look for things we could get done ourselves, by organizing.

Here is an example. There were several terrible tenements on West Twenty-second Street, owned by two guys who, simply put, were slumlords. A lot of people living in these buildings had been placed there by the Division of AIDS Services. (DAS provides key support for city residents living with HIV and AIDS, ranging from referral to support groups and medical providers, to help with finding housing and financial resources.) Even though these owners were getting a ton of money in rent from the city to house people living with HIV and AIDS, they were providing extremely substandard living conditions. This was a perennial problem, and unfortunately it still exists to some degree.

So we organized what turned out to be a multiyear effort to get them to clear up the violations on their buildings or to sell them to responsible owners, which is what they eventually were forced to do. This campaign lasted for so long that we were still working on it by the time I took over Tom's seat on the City Council.

After I was elected, we got a local morning television news show, *Good Day New York*, to do a story about how these awful landlords weren't providing heat in the dead of winter. We arranged to do the story in the freezing-cold apartment of a DAS client in one of these buildings. I showed up at the apartment at five-thirty or six a.m., and he had the kitchen stove blasting heat because he didn't want it to be cold for the television crew!

He was being considerate to us and the crew. I said, "Turn off
the stove! Open the windows!" We couldn't do a story about a
freezing apartment if it was eighty degrees inside!

Another citywide issue I got involved in through Tom's
office back in the day still isn't resolved: New York City's
annual St. Patrick's Day Parade. When Tom was first running for office in 1991, the Irish Lesbian and Gay Organization (ILGO) applied to be a contingent in the parade, but its
application was denied on ostensibly procedural grounds that
made no sense at all. Procedure was obviously not the real
issue. The people who run the parade, the Ancient Order
of Hibernians, see it as a Catholic parade. They don't want
LGBT people included in any visible way. The fact that ac-
tively Irish LGBT people exist didn't make any difference
to them. Lawsuits followed, and the Hibernians have not
budged in the two decades since.

Once Tom was elected, for the first St. Patrick's Day he
was in office, he didn't march. At that time, for an elected official of any kind, let alone one of Irish ancestry, not to march
was a big statement. After that we asked elected officials to
pledge not to march as long as ILGO was banned. Most affirmatively signed the pledge and said, "I won't march." Others
didn't sign, then just didn't march, and still don't march. And
statewide elected officials often find a way to be off in a far
corner of the state on St. Patrick's Day.

Over the decades, we offered many compromises in response to their stated objections: You don't want a contingent
behind an identifiable LGBT banner? Forget banners! We'd
march behind the City Council banner. Sashes are a big thing
in the parade—people wear ones with the name of the county
they or their families are from. So LGBT people could wear
a rainbow sash. Or they could wear a sticker with a shamrock
on top of a pink triangle. In 2007 my father, Kim, a contingent
of councilmembers and Irish American activists, and I were
invited to march as a group in Dublin's official St. Patrick's
Day Parade wearing those exact stickers. We were trying to
come up with *some* identifiable way marching would work in
New York. Think of it—it's okay in Dublin, but not on Fifth
Avenue. Sadly, nothing so far has worked. I'm hoping that the
next generation of AOH leadership will come to a fair compromise, so we can put this issue behind us. But for now, you won't
find me marching in the city's annual St. Patrick's Day Parade.

During my time with Tom, one extremely contentious
citywide issue got resolved; it involved an unexpected and
very high-profile battle with the city's newly elected and
combative mayor, Rudolph Giuliani. One of the first things
Giuliani wanted to do after taking office was to eliminate the
Division of AIDS Services. I don't think the mayor had any
idea that his plan to kill DAS would cause such an uproar,
and in the beginning I'm not sure he appreciated the significance of DAS or the essential services it provided. Maybe
he just saw it as an easy thing to cut from the budget. I don't
think he thought it was going to be a citywide battle.

We found out about Giuliani's plans from a source inside City Hall, and we passed the information right along to the media. This was on a Thursday, and on the following Monday we had literally thousands of people outside City Hall protesting the plan (and this was before the days of the Internet). The mayor wasn't the kind of person to back down, so the protest turned into a huge citywide effort to prevent him from eliminating DAS. After an unyielding battle, we prevailed, and the City Council later passed Local Law 49, codifying DAS. This prevented Giuliani from eliminating DAS, and made it so that any future mayor who wants to get rid of it will have to get the City Council to repeal the law.

What I learned from that experience, and from all my time with Tom, was that if you want to get things done— whether it's finding a way to fix up crappy tenements so people can live with dignity, or getting legislation passed to protect vital city programs—then you've got to work hard and be creative. And you have to be willing to work hard in a way that's relevant to the particular situation. Sometimes that means doing tons of research, sometimes it's meeting with different people who won't talk to each other, sometimes it's participating in activities or organizing events, and sometimes it's coordinating with other staff or experts or elected officials. Ultimately, the people who succeed in getting the city to be a better place are the ones who are the most focused and work the hardest. It's a lesson I carry with me every day.

CHAPTER 8

Facing Myself

I came to trust Tom in a way I had never trusted anyone in my life. He was so up-front and open about himself in every way, including the fact that he was a recovering alcoholic. And because he spoke about himself so honestly, he gave the impression that he didn't judge other people. People would tell him things about their lives that they might not consider telling anyone else. I had felt comfortable enough to tell Tom that I was gay, not that it was a realistic option to hide my relationship with Laura. But now as we started a new stage of working together, I felt the need to tell him my darkest secret.

One day a few months after the primary, when I was his chief of staff, we were working alone together, and he started talking about bulimia. Maybe he brought it up because he thought I had a problem. But once he opened the door, I decided to step through it and told him something I'd never mentioned to another soul.

"Oh, I do that," I said. At that point, I had been making myself sick for ten years, since I was sixteen, when my mother was dying. I would think, *I feel bad. I need not to feel bad.* Then I would overeat to feel better or less sad. I would think, *If I make myself sick, afterward I won't feel bad for some period of time.* That's what was going on subconsciously.

But I told myself that I was doing it because I was fat and wanted to lose weight. It was my way to eat and try to lose weight at the same time. When you're young, you don't have any sense that you're trying to get relief from feeling emotionally overwhelmed, or from the fact that your life has become unmanageable (although that's clearly what I was after). Instead, you tell yourself it's all about losing weight. No matter how many times I told myself I needed to stop doing it, the brief sense of relief I got afterward would become incentive enough to keep on doing it. The problem was that over time the relief I got became less and less. But by then you really can't stop—it is such a compulsion. I knew I had a problem because I wanted to stop, but as much as I tried to, I couldn't. I'd say to myself, *Tomorrow I'm not going to,* or *This week I'm not going to,* and then I'd do it again.

It was disappointing and frustrating, so it was something of a relief to confide in someone I trusted. Tom was kind and supportive, but he was also concerned. He didn't press me, but in the weeks and months that followed, he encouraged me to seek treatment. He explained that like all addictive diseases, bulimia is progressive. He recommended that I go to an inpatient eating disorder clinic and suggested a place where someone he knew had gone.

If it had come from anybody else, I would have rejected the idea, but Tom was the right messenger. I didn't welcome the idea of checking into a clinic, but he helped me recognize that the only way I could get better was to get help, and that the best way to get help was in a clinical setting.

Tom told everyone at work that I was taking a leave of absence. My girlfriend, Laura, of course knew I was going, and I told a couple of friends. But that was it. Once I was there, I called my sister to tell her where I was and why, and her response was very positive. I never told my father.

I remember getting off the plane and looking for the person with the sign for the clinic. A couple of other people were getting picked up at the same time, and once we got to the place, we were each taken into a different room to fill out lots of paperwork and answer lots of questions. Then I got my room assignment. We had the rest of the day to settle in, and things didn't really start until the next morning.

My first morning didn't get off to a great start. Because it's a medical facility and they keep track of your health while you're in treatment, they draw blood on a regular basis. The first time I just about fainted. Not full-out fainting, but on the way to fainting, which is something that rarely happens to me. I must have been very anxious, and the needle in my arm just pushed me over the edge.

Every day in rehab was pretty structured. You got up, you had breakfast, and you had individual therapy, where you had to talk about yourself, or maybe group therapy, where you had to talk about yourself and listen to other people talking about themselves. There might be exercise walks, and there might be journaling. Those of us with eating disorders sat together and ate together, sometimes under the supervision of a staff member. This structure made it possible for us to understand our issues better and break bad patterns. It was a good start.

We also got an education on nutrition. Having grown up in a home where our meals were determined by the route home from the day's lessons, I found the new information confusing but critical—and it has been useful ever since. That said, learning about the difference between a carbohydrate and a protein was a breeze compared with the therapy sessions. You had to talk about your life in at least one one-on-one therapy session and in one group session a day. The whole process was incredibly challenging because for the first time I was forced to face elements of myself that I had ignored.

People came to rehab with all sorts of issues and goals. One enormously overweight woman just wanted to be able to walk on the beach with her grandchildren and to bend down and pick up shells. A very overweight man in his thirties had the kinds of health problems you might expect in someone decades older. An anorexic mom talked a lot about her children, and how she felt bad about what she was putting them through. What struck me about these people was the fact that they just wanted to be able to do the simplest things, walking with a grandchild on the beach or being normal about food at home. Our shared challenges were making our lives complicated and unmanageable. We all yearned for a time when these issues would fade, where something or someone greater than ourselves could help us help ourselves, so we could get on with our lives in the fullest ways possible.

Everyone talked about trying this and that and the other thing to stop doing whatever it was that had landed them in rehab. Even if their experiences were different from mine, I could identify with the feelings they were going through. It helped that everybody was there for the same basic mission, so the kinship and camaraderie made opening up a little easier.

I talked a lot about my childhood and my mother and those feelings of responsibility, guilt, and blame. I believed—and I guess I'll always believe it on some level—that it was my fault she got sick, that it's my fault she died, that if I had been a better child, if I had been an easier child, she wouldn't have gotten sick, or the sickness would not have progressed and she would not have died.

I think when you're a kid, you need to assign blame to

something or someone, because otherwise you're just living in a universe that's spinning out of control. Now, all that is intellectually absurd, and even at sixteen you know that that's not how cancer works. I wasn't a bad kid, but knowing something rationally and intellectually is different from understanding the implications and impact of those feelings on your life, and when something starts in childhood in a dark and bad time, it can be hard, if not impossible, to break that cycle without help. I came to realize that even though I was in my midtwenties, I was dealing with issues of my childhood.

It was one of my first significant or big moments of asking for help. It was a shock for me to let go of the idea that "I can do it all, I can fix it—it's all on me." This perspective had become part of me growing up, when I was taking care of people. So that message was significant for me to hear and take in.

Another important thing happened: I realized that it's okay to not feel good about yourself. It's not the end of the world, but you have to find ways to cope with that feeling and to let go of it so you don't internalize it. Because if you're bulimic or drinking too much, you're making yourself feel worse. This may seem completely obvious, but sometimes it's hard to see.

Probably a third thing was the recognition that when things happen in life, they have an impact. It's no use pretending they don't, because they do. They don't go away so you have to deal with them. I had to learn that confronting them is not an admission of weakness or failure, which is how I'd thought about it before. I wasn't dealing with it properly. I started to piece it together during that month. Rehab planted seeds in me that then grew later on.

When I went to rehab, it had a food wing and an alcohol and drug wing. We did some things together and some things separately. The clinic basically said that if you're in either wing, food or drink, you have an addictive personality, so if you drink, you really should think about stopping. In the time after rehab, I started thinking about how I drank, and that I often drank for the sake of getting drunk. I had thought it was normal, but I came to realize it wasn't. As the years went by, I started drinking much less, cutting back, watching what I drank, never drinking to get drunk. And then about three years ago, I decided, look, if you're spending time managing it and thinking so much about controlling it, it's not a good or healthy thing. So I asked for help, and I got it. Over the last three years I haven't drank at all. And the truth is, my realizations at the rehab clinic over two decades ago started a process that has now fully come to fruition.

You would think that given my family history I should have been more aware of my potential for having a drinking problem. My father's grandfather was a terrible drunk, and consequently my father's father, Pa Quinn, didn't drink, and he drilled into my father that drinking was a bad thing. This was a story my father told repeatedly throughout my childhood. So my father didn't drink, and he was very up-front about it being a practical thing; he had no philosophical or religious reasoning for not drinking or for why he thought it was a bad thing.

My father's mother, Nana Quinn, drank too much, too, and so did my mother's father and one of his brothers, who were always being shipped off to the drunk tank to sober up. My mother drank too much as well, although it was hard to tell if she was on alcohol or the calming-down pills the doctors gave her. But none of that penetrated, and once I started going out to clubs and dances, I'd always drink until I was drunk.

I did not have any expectations of finding a cure or discovering happiness by going to rehab. I was just looking for freedom from misery. If I could simply feel neutral, that would be achieving a state of bliss. I didn't have to be happy, just not feel horrible. It was a modest goal, and by the time I went back to work, I didn't feel horrible, although it would be a long and difficult road before I felt good, even happy.

But the amazing news is that today I actually know happiness, and know that even in life's dark moments I can get help. It's okay to ask for it. Those miracles that my mother and Aunt Julia believed in—if you pray, if you work on yourself, if you know when to pray and when to run—those miracles can and do come true.

CHAPTER 9

City Council

I stayed with Tom as his chief of staff for nearly six years. It got to the point where I could have done the job with my eyes closed, and I needed a change. Leaving it wasn't easy, especially because with Tom I had no secrets, but it was time. The job was getting too easy. And when things get too easy, you don't do them as well. That's not fair to anybody.

Tom was supportive and encouraged me to reach for something that would be more challenging. "You need to make your mark in the world, separate and apart from me," he said. And he was right. I needed to do something new. But where was I to go? It would have been great to move up at City Hall, but with Giuliani in office, I could forget about a job on the mayor's staff (and I wouldn't have wanted one given our dramatically divergent political views), so I looked outside city government.

I eventually landed a job as executive director of the New York City Gay & Lesbian Anti-Violence Project. I'd worked with AVP when I was on Tom's staff and had a lot of respect for them. They were a good mix of providing direct service and counseling crime victims, and also doing advocacy—trying to change and improve things in the police department. I liked the variety, and I liked the fact that the group's activities were informed by the real-life experiences of their clients. The closer the work is to the clients, the more you understand their problems and the challenges everybody faces.

Hate crimes were even more rampant then, and AVP played an important role in bringing attention to the problem. During this period our community endured a series of attacks, including murders. These can be challenging crimes to deal with, because if an LGBT person is murdered and wasn't out, how does the family go to the police about a hate crime? Very often the family would say to AVP, "Don't say anything" about the fact that the person was gay. But the family really wasn't our client. Still, despite the stigma, mothers and/or fathers would come to us in search of justice or eventually join in the effort.

When I took over at AVP, my goal was to expand the great work they had done and to enlist the community to put even more pressure on the police department, the district attorney's offices, and Mayor Giuliani to make the city safer for LGBT people. By now I understood the workings of city government and knew how to get it to pay attention and even follow through. I knew we could fix this by building bridges between our communities and the people in power. For example, back then the police weren't as well-trained or sensitive about same-sex domestic violence and sexual assault as they are now, and consequently the police weren't always as responsive as they needed to be, but that's gotten so much better because of everyone's work.

Another one of my objectives as AVP's executive director was to build on the organization's already good relationship with the police, and to help them do a better job recognizing and acknowledging hate crimes. Sometimes it was easy, and sometimes it wasn't. For example, one time it seemed obvious that we were dealing with a hate crime, but at first the police refused to classify it as one.

A couple of guys were walking home in West Chelsea, crossing Twenty-third Street and heading north to Twenty-fifth Street. A turning car got too close to them, and the guys yelled something at the people in the car. Then the guys in the car yelled something anti-LGBT at them. They got out of the car and chased the guys down Twenty-third Street, up Tenth Avenue, and across Twenty-fifth Street. They caught one of the men and beat him over the head. He lost an eye.

The police department chose not to categorize this as a hate crime, because it began as a traffic altercation. Of course that was ridiculous. There are lots of traffic incidents, and 99.99 percent of them don't end up with people getting chased and beaten up, much less losing an eye.

In response to the police department's failure to categorize this incident as a hate crime, we organized demonstrations and did press conferences, calling on the police to reverse that decision. We held a demonstration in front of the local police precinct. On a local television news show, I debated the commanding officer of the NYPD's Hate Crimes Task Force over what constituted a hate crime. Eventually everyone's work made a big difference, and the NYPD changed its mind. This matters because if government and society don't name a crime accurately, it is as if it never happened.

Same-sex domestic violence is another key area of work and service for AVP. Recently a woman came up to me at an event and said, "I know you from AVP. You moved me out of my apartment, and saved me." I immediately remembered her. She had come to AVP because she was a victim of domestic violence. Her girlfriend hadn't been home, so we went there and packed all the woman's possessions in shopping bags and garbage bags and moved her out. Then the girlfriend cross-complained, resulting in both of them getting arrested. I went and waited for the woman at the station house until she was released. The next week she came to the office for counseling. We saw a car parked out front, and the ex-girlfriend was in it. Since she had orders of protection, we called the Sixth Precinct, and they came and arrested the ex-girlfriend. Seeing this woman, who is now married and has a child, made me so proud of my work and the work of all the staff of AVP. It reminded me of how critical the interactions between government and citizenry are, especially when people need help and support.

Three years into my time at AVP, a state senate seat opened up, and Tom Duane started talking about running for it. So naturally I started thinking about running for his seat on the City Council. I felt a little guilty, because I hadn't been at AVP for long, and becoming an elected official had not always been a huge goal of mine. But I was definitely interested. I knew that Tom's support would be exceedingly helpful. I went back and forth, but the more I thought about it, the more appealing it became. I could play a role in the deliberations of the City Council. As Tom's chief of staff, I had learned the nuts and bolts of advocating for our neighborhood, but as an elected member of the City Council, I could take the lead in a way that I couldn't as chief of staff.

Soon after I made my decision, I announced that I'd be running in the February 1999 special election to fill Tom's seat. (Tom ran for the open state senate seat basically unopposed and easily won.) Not unexpectedly, several other people decided to run for Tom's council seat as well. Christopher Lynn had been commissioner for both the Department of Transportation and the Taxi and Limousine Commission under Giuliani; Aubrey Lees was a Democratic district leader in Greenwich Village. Both were openly gay. Carlos Manzano, a Democratic state committeeman and president of the McManus Democratic Club, wasn't specific about his sexual orientation. And we also had a write-in candidate who was the only openly heterosexual candidate in the race.

On the issues, all of us basically had the same positions, so I ran on my experience as a housing organizer, community activist, and Tom's chief of staff. I got endorsements from most of the key elected officials and community leaders in the district. And I inherited some of Tom's state senate race campaign staff, which had just elected him. We wound up winning by a significant margin.

How could I experience this amazing event in my life without thinking of my mother? She had been with me for only sixteen years, but in some ways she is with me every day. She had a devout, spiritual belief that people have an obligation to help one another. She believed that—along with raising her children—her life's work was helping people in need. She believed, in some almost divine sense, that we are not allowed to leave people behind. Maybe because she knew that she wasn't going to live as long as she wanted, she was determined to use her time as aggressively as she could, to make as big an impact as she could. Her sense of urgency has become a big part of my personality.

My mother also made it abundantly clear to my sister and me, and this was in the 1960s and 1970s, that we could be whatever we wanted to be, and that we were to be the best at whatever we chose to be. She imbued in us a strong belief about the power of girls and women. As I've said, on her dresser she had a little altar with statues and relics and medals of women, and Elizabeth Ann Seton was her favorite saint. She believed devoutly in the power of women to bring miraculous interventions. Today Ellen and I can't do miracles, but we have done what we wanted, and we have done it well.

I decided I wanted my swearing-in ceremony for City Council to be women-focused and fun and edgy, maybe a little edgier than my mother would have expected. My friend Victoria Cruz was the emcee. Vickie had been a client at AVP, and she's transgender. She was in the welfare-to-work program and was assigned to work in a nursing home, which she loved. She would have been very good at her job. When some of the other nurses realized she was transgender, she became a target. She bravely reported that a group of nurses had groped her and used anti-gay slurs against her. Her case was serious. A criminal court eventually found two of the nurses guilty of harassment. She spent so much time in our office that she basically became the receptionist, so we eventually hired her as the receptionist. Today she is a caseworker at AVP. As I said, she was the emcee of my swearing-in ceremony. Marie Wilson from the Ms. Foundation was the keynote speaker, and Eve Ensler performed a scene from *The*

Vagina Monologues as free entertainment. The daughter of friends held the book I used to take the oath of office. My poor father was onstage as Eve started the *Vagina Monologues* excerpt. It was a bit more graphic than I'd expected. When she was done, my dad looked at me and said, "You couldn't just have had the Pledge of Allegiance?"

I can't remember if I spoke about my mom that day, but she was there in spirit. She would have loved it. She would have had her hair done and worn a great outfit and her good jewelry. Seeing me sworn in to the City Council would have pleased her, because now I was in a position to help make life better for the people in my district and for all New Yorkers. I think my mother would have been happy that both of her daughters chose careers they enjoy.

The City Council is the legislative branch, and the mayor is the executive branch of New York City's government. As the legislative body, we have power over all the city's administrative laws and codes. The mayor proposes the budget, but we have to negotiate it together and come to agreement and vote on it. All the big decisions around zoning, and what gets built, and how things get built are the result of negotiations between the mayor and the council.

After I had a couple of years on the council, I set my sights on becoming chair of its health committee, which has jurisdiction over a range of issues that affect people in the most fundamental ways. The Speaker of the City Council, who was then Gifford Miller, decides on committee chairs.

I'd lobbied Gifford to become chair of the health committee and was appointed in January 2002.

While Gifford was running for Speaker I'd supported him, and I traveled around the city helping him win support. This work helped me in creating the health committee agenda. For example, we spent a decent amount of time on Staten Island, which helped me focus on the fact that while Staten Island has some big private hospitals, it is the only borough without a public hospital. In a lot of ways its residents are underserved in public health, particularly those who are not insured. Early on in my chairpersonship, there was a proposal to close one of the island's private hospitals. We tried to save the hospital but couldn't. The next question was then how to deal with the health-care needs of the residents of the island's North Shore. We built a coalition and worked with lots of folks and were able to open a federally qualified health center to fill part of the gap. When I was chair, we studied the length of wait times for screening mammograms across the city and released a report that compared wait times for private and public hospitals. Staten Island has a particularly high rate of breast cancer but no public hospital. So Minority Leader Jimmy Oddo and I had the city buy a mammogram van that focuses exclusively on Staten Island, because uninsured people have nowhere on the island to go. Health care is such a significant issue out there.

As chair of the health committee I had to deal with a lot of controversial and important issues, including Mayor

Michael Bloomberg's proposal to ban smoking in all restaurants and bars. Bloomberg is fiercely antismoking and saw this as an issue of workplace safety: he thought people who worked in restaurants and bars should be free from tobacco smoke just as office workers already were. In 1995 New York City passed a law that outlawed smoking in restaurants with more than thirty-five seats, although not in the bar areas of all restaurants and not in stand-alone bars. As a result of the new law, thirteen thousand restaurants and bars across the city banned smoking.

Lots of people greeted the mayor's proposal as radical. In New York State, restaurants were required to set aside 70 percent of their seating area for nonsmokers, but the smoking area could be in the same room, which if you think about it is ridiculous if you're trying to protect nonsmokers from secondhand smoke.

I tried to do everything I could to ensure the bill's passage—I was its lead sponsor. Not surprisingly, it was a pretty high-pitched battle, because many restaurant and bar owners thought a smoking ban was going to be bad for business. They were worried about their financial future.

Despite how heated the process got, it didn't intimidate me, even though at times it could feel endless, especially after hours-long public hearings where everyone had an opportunity to speak their mind. It's hard to predict what will matter to people, but when something does, you have to give them the chance to be heard. So we had tons of meetings with every constituent group, and we listened to their perspectives on what a total ban on smoking in their bars would mean for them and for their livelihoods. At the end of the process, which appropriately took months, most of the opponents were still opposed to it, but no one complained about the process, and many even thanked the council for it, because it had given them an opportunity to make their voices heard.

I learned an important lesson from this experience: how you do things matters. There's a difference between giving people an opportunity to be heard and giving people what they want. People want what they want, but they also respect being listened to. This is something I always try to be mindful of, although sometimes I get in a rush and forget. I know it matters in terms of how people feel about our work in the City Council and throughout city government. Even if they do not agree with what we've done, at least they have been shown respect. In any case, the smoking ban proved to be a success. It caused no decrease in revenues at restaurants or bars. None of the understandable fears came to pass, and given New York City's prominence, I like to think that our ban had a ripple effect.

As health chair, I intervened to prevent a strike by thousands of home health aides, by pushing their employer and their union to meet and come to an agreement. In the end neither side got exactly what it wanted, but the deal was good enough for everyone to walk away from the negotiating table feeling like they'd gotten *something*. I have a soft spot in my heart for home health aides. They work so hard caring for our family members, like my mother, and I will always be grateful to the women who were so kind to my mother in her last months.

I'm not sure where or how, but sometime during those early years, I found a way to negotiate so that more often than not we ended up with a deal, not a standoff. I just don't stop or take no for an answer, and I try as hard as I can to keep everyone at the negotiating table. I believe there is almost always a moment in the deliberations when the different sides will intersect, creating a moment of commonality. If you're watching and listening carefully, people will unknowingly offer you that moment. They'll say something more honest than what they've been saying for hours before. It will show what they really want and need, as opposed to what they have been saying they want and need. You have to wait for that moment, and then seize on it, and then anything is possible.

I came to understand that the personal is never wholly separate from the political. We are most moved by the issues that touch our lives and our hearts. When I joined the council, I didn't know that my heart was about to be moved in the most amazing way.

CHAPTER 10

Kim

By the time I was elected to the City Council, my relationship with Laura was over. We are still friends, and I'm very grateful to her for helping me take the biggest step in my personal life. But now I was living alone again, and I went back to telling myself that not everyone gets everything in life. I gave up on the possibility of having another significant relationship and accepted that it wasn't in the cards for me. As confident as I was in my ability to help solve my constituents' problems, I had no confidence that I'd ever find a real partner in life. Then in the summer of 2001 my friend Emily Giske got inspired to play matchmaker when she spotted me, looking sad and lonely, in a nail salon in Greenwich Village.

I had gone for a manicure to try to cheer myself up after the death of my dear friend Ruth Kahn. Ruth was a sharp-tongued, chain-smoking neighborhood activist who was like a second mom to me. In fact, she was everybody's bossy Jewish mother, butting into your life and telling you what to wear, what to do, what to support, and what to oppose. She was short, really small, but you never thought of her that way, because she was always pointing and wagging her finger in your face.

When I was working on Tom Duane's campaign, Ruth was one of a core group of political people who were always organizing something or fighting someone or mad about this or that. Every day she would come around the campaign office to help, and you'd get the Ruth Kahn download. She expressed her opinions in a forceful and entertaining way, as in "A fence around a park gives new f——ing meaning to open space." She hated fences around parks.

After Tom was elected to the City Council, Ruth took me shopping, because on campaigns you wear jeans and T-shirts, and she didn't want me showing up at City Hall as his chief of staff "dressed like a slob." For a retired social worker in her seventies, she had quite the "out there" fashion sense; she wore leather pants because they were warm, or so she said—I think she wore them because she could. And for some reason, I didn't mind her telling me what to wear. Ruth was a complete character, totally opinionated and loyal and loving in an obnoxious and pushy way—a great friend and a real constant in my life. And then suddenly in 2001 she was gone. A massive heart attack.

Her death was devastating to me. I had no appetite and lost weight without trying. I must have looked pretty bad when Emily saw me at the salon. It was probably a good thing she didn't have anyone to introduce me to that day, because I think I'd have said no. But a short time later Emily and her girlfriend were in Provincetown, where they wound up spending time with Kim Catullo, whom they had met the previous March and liked a lot. At some point Emily decided to be a matchmaker.

Kim had only recently moved to the city from New Jersey, where she grew up and worked as an attorney. Like me, Kim had lost her mother when she was a teenager. So Emily made a pitch to Kim about what we had in common. When she mentioned that I was a politician, though, that was it. Kim wasn't interested in going out with an elected official. She's a private person, and being with someone in the public eye was precisely what she *wasn't* interested in. She actually loves politics and studied political science at Rutgers University, but she is a private person.

Not long after Emily told her about me, Kim was out for a run the week before the Democratic primary in 2001. She jogged across Christopher Street, and every telephone pole had a campaign poster with me, Tom Duane, and others on it. She decided I was kind of cute. She called Emily to tell her she was okay about being fixed up with me for a date.

Emily was particularly excited, because while Kim had been on vacation in Provincetown that summer with Emily, she'd noticed a woman with red hair and joked the whole time that Emily should find her "redheaded woman." So at least I had *that* going for me!

So Emily called me and made her pitch: that Kim was attractive, a partner at a law firm, self-made, smart, and kind. She sounded interesting, and I didn't have anything to lose, so I said yes. The four of us arranged to meet at a Village bar and restaurant, on a Saturday, but Emily and her girlfriend had to cancel. The dinner that didn't happen was scheduled for September 8, 2001. You know what happened three days later.

Nobody can forget it. It was overwhelmingly sad and terrifying. In an instant, out of nowhere, a tragedy visited our city and our people. It was the most beautiful day, warm and dry, with a sky of bright but deep blue. But, now, when those of us who lived through it in New York City look up and see a perfect blue sky and feel the warm air, we don't remember a gorgeous day, we say, "It's just like 9/11."

That day members of my staff and friends came up to my apartment in Chelsea, and we watched and wept, just as everybody else did. In the days following 9/11, everyone was trying to make sense of it, and no one wanted to be alone. Everybody wanted to be with friends and family.

Reports show that, in the months that followed, people were inspired by September 11 to take a new look at their lives. Some people ended relationships. Others started them. It just so happened that my first date with Kim was the start of the most important relationship in my life.

Three days after the attack, I was out with my father delivering dust masks to senior centers in Chelsea when Emily called to suggest dinner that night with her girlfriend and Kim. I got to the restaurant, and the three of them were sitting at a table by the front window. Kim remembers that I came in like a typical politician and gave her a firm handshake and introduced myself as if I were running for office. Really I was just nervous and was having trouble looking at Kim because I found her so attractive. Her pretty brown eyes drew me in, and she had beautiful, shoulder-length dark hair. Later, Emily said she couldn't believe that either of us even showed up, because we're both so shy in this kind of context.

In the middle of dinner, we all went outside to participate in a candlelight vigil and sang "God Bless America." The president had declared September 14 a National Day of Prayer and Remembrance, and there were all kinds of events across the country and around the world. So there were people standing on the sidewalk up and down Eighth Avenue, and we all held candles and sang. Then the next night a whole group of us went out to dinner and then to Bowlmor Lanes for some bowling. Our first date alone happened the following Wednesday, at the Red Cat in Chelsea.

We had a cozy table against the wall with a candle off to the side that made Kim's eyes sparkle. The conversation was so natural and easy that by the time dessert arrived, I felt comfortable asking Kim to tell me the story about what happened to her mother. "I know you lost your mother," I said, "and I would like to know the story." Kim said she didn't think that was appropriate for a first official date and that it had been really sad, but I looked at her across the table and said very softly, "No, I've been through it, too, and it would really mean a lot to me to know."

Kim was one of five children, but because she was by far the youngest, she grew up like an only child—something like my sister and me. Her twin brothers are seventeen years older, her sister is thirteen years older, and her other brother is nine years older. Kim was fifteen when her mother was diagnosed with uterine cancer, but she had surgery and chemotherapy, which put her into full remission. Then two years later, just three days before Christmas, she developed a cough, and they thought she had a flu or pneumonia, so they put her in the hospital. She died a very short time later.

At this point in the story, the waitress came over and asked us if everything was okay because our dessert had melted into a puddle in the middle of the plate—we hadn't touched it. I told her everything was fine, and as soon as she walked away, Kim told me her mother died on Christmas Day. She had been looking down at the table until then, and when she looked up, she could see that my eyes were filled with tears. "See, I told you we shouldn't have talked about it," she said. "It's not really a great date subject."

And I said to her, "No, it's not that. It's just that I thought I had the saddest story ever, because my mother died on December 21 and was buried on Christmas Eve— Until I heard *your* story . . ."

The loss of our mothers hit both of us really hard but also gave us a powerful bond with each other. So few people really know what it's like to lose your mother as a teenager, and here it had happened to both of us basically at the same age. And because we were by far the youngest in our families, we were left alone with our fathers, who had to step into shoes that were impossible to fill. We both understood, without having to explain, all about Christmas. It had been huge for both our families, and both our mothers drove that with the preparations, the gifts, the decorations, and the parties. It's a time of year when everybody is supposed to be happy, but it had been tainted forever by something that was so sad and painful.

Once our mothers were gone, Christmas was never the same; it became a sad anniversary. Now Kim and I celebrate it together. Of course we remember our mothers, and we have our moments, but Christmas is something we've been able to give back to each other because we understand and don't have to pretend to be happy every second of the season. We *are* happy because we have each other, because we can celebrate together, and because we know what a struggle it was to get here.

Our next date was set for September 21, but I had to push back the time because I had agreed to attend a rally in

Madison Square Park in support of Muslim New Yorkers. This rally was important to me. After 9/11, anticipating a terrible backlash against Muslims, I had visited a number of mosques to see the imams and members of their congregations. I wanted to make sure they knew that people in the city government embraced them as members of our New York family and in no way associated them with the attacks. I offered my reassurance that we were there to support them and left my card in case they needed anything or thought I could be of help.

But hate crimes targeting the Muslim community were already occurring in New York City and around the country. So when the Muslim community organized a small rally in Madison Square Park decrying them, I was asked to speak. I felt it was very important to make a statement that the worst response to the attack on the World Trade Center would be for us to turn against one another. That was exactly what the terrorists had wanted, and we weren't going to let it happen.

After the rally, I joined Kim and Emily and her girl-friend at a local restaurant. Kim had met them for a drink, and when I got there, we left. Our original plan had been to go to the movies, but I decided to invite Kim to my place to watch the huge benefit concert for the World Trade Center first responders on TV. Millions of people all over the world participated in that event. All kinds of stars and musicians and famous people came, from Billy Joel and Bruce Springsteen to Alicia Keys and Jon Bon Jovi.

Before we watched the concert, we walked my dog, Andy, and I was relieved to discover that Kim is a dog person. And afterward we talked some more. Before things went any further, I thought Kim should know some things about me. I wasn't proud of them, and I wasn't sure she'd want to be with me once she knew about them. "There's something I want to tell you," I said. "I have issues." She said, "Okay, everyone has issues." I told her that I had a problem with alcohol and bulimia and had spent a month in rehab years before. Much to my relief, she was supportive and nice—not shocked at all. I'd shared these secrets that I thought were potential deal-breakers, but instead she was lovely about them.

Then it was Kim's turn to share something she thought *I* should know about. She said she wasn't out to anybody, that nobody at work or in her family knew she was gay. Without thinking, I threw up my hands and said in a too-loud voice, "*That's* a problem!"

She was shocked. "You just told me all these things about yourself, about your issues, and I tell you this one thing, and that's a problem? You're kidding, right?"

You'd think I'd have backed down at that point, but I didn't. "No, I'm serious!" I said.

Then I started laughing, and Kim started laughing, because we both realized how ridiculous I sounded.

It's absurd how insensitive I was. I had struggled for years just to accept myself as a lesbian, let alone share that information. When we spoke that night in 2001, it had been only ten years since I'd come out to my colleagues and my father. And only thirteen since my first crush had left me determined to keep tight control over totally unwelcome feelings. I felt different now, but it was important for me to remember the long and difficult road I had traveled to get to the point in my life where I felt reasonably comfortable having people know I was gay. What could I have been thinking?

There was one point of difference that didn't take me long to resolve. I used to be a Mets fan, because I grew up on Long Island. On our third date Kim asked, "Are you a Yankees or a Mets fan?" because she's a crazed Yankees fan. And I said, "I'm a Mets fan. It'll be so funny, a two-family home." And in all seriousness she said, "Look, I want to be perfectly clear, I am not willing to go any further with a Mets fan." I dumped the Mets in a hot second.

Things with Kim moved crazy fast. It was like the old joke: *What do lesbians bring on a second date? A U-Haul.* It wasn't *that* fast, but after the fourth date, I think we both knew we were a couple. And just a month or so later we bought each other commitment rings of silver. We were both thirty-five and knew we wanted to build a life and a family and a home together. The rings symbolized our love and our lifetime commitment to each other. Not marriage, because at the time legal marriage was so beyond the realm of possibility for a lesbian couple that we didn't even think about it.

Around this time, Kim invited me out to New Jersey to one of her family events, of which there are many throughout the year. The Catullos get together for just about every occasion, rotating from house to house. For my introduction to the Catullo family, we went to Kim's brother's house for her sister-in-law's birthday. Everyone was there—siblings, grandchildren, in-laws, nieces and nephews, and Kim's father—maybe twenty people in all. The only one missing was Kim's brother Anthony, one of the twins, who was away at a football game. Kim told her family she was bringing a friend, which she'd done in the past, so there was absolutely no pressure on her or me.

Kim's family embraced me immediately, and I fit right in. They're loud, fun, boisterous, and physically demonstrative. They kiss and hug everybody hello and good-bye. I'd always wanted a big family, and now I had one, and I loved it. From the first they included me in conversations, the ribbing, the cooking—not my strong suit, but I was good for appetizers and dessert when they asked me to bring something. Kim says her family loves me more than they love her, which of course is not true, but I couldn't have hoped for a more embracing and loving in-law family, and that included Kim's father. Early on he told Kim, "I'm glad you have Chris."

Our fathers have a lot in common. They both served in the Pacific during World War II. They're the same age. They talk about the war, their old neighborhoods, and how life has changed, and about what's in the newspaper. Down at our shore house, they spend a lot of time sitting on the porch

Just married! My parents, Larry and Mary Callaghan Quinn, on their wedding day at Good Shepherd Church, Inwood, New York, June 14, 1952.

All dressed up with my family on the boardwalk at Rockaway Beach, Queens, New York, January 1968. *From left to right:* Aunt Julia, my mom, and my grandparents, John and Nellie Callaghan.

A stylish threesome on
Fifth Avenue in 1971,
with my aunt, Julia
(left), and my sister,
Ellen *(right)*.

With my mother at my home
away from home, the Glen View
Farms stables in Glen Head,
New York, in the mid-1970s.

At a horse show
my sister was in
in the late 1970s.

My father and I managed a little sightseeing while looking at colleges in Maine in the summer of 1983.

Who is that under all those feathers? Dressed up as the Bantam, the Trinity College mascot, Hartford, Connecticut, mid-1980s.

With my father on graduation day at Trinity College, 1988.

While I was executive director of the New York City Gay and Lesbian
Anti-Violence Project, I held a joint news conference with then City
Councilman Tom Duane to raise the alarm about an increase in anti-gay
violence, June 1998.

On a Hudson River pier in Chelsea with my friend
Wayne Kawadler and our coparented dog, Andy, 1998.

We won! Celebrating my first election to the City Council with my political consultant, Mark Guma *(far left),* and Maura Keaney, my campaign manager, February 16, 1999.

It's official! The 1999 swearing-in for new members of the City Council. *From left to right, with hands raised:* Michael Nelson, James Oddo, and me. Witnessing are former City Council Minority Leader Thomas Ognibene *(far left)* and the former Speaker of the City Council Peter Vallone Sr. *(far right).*

Marching in the New York City LGBT Pride parade during Hillary Clinton's first run for the United States Senate in June 2000. It was like being with a rock star! *From left to right:* former mayor Ed Koch (deceased), State Assemblyman Richard Gottfried, former City Councilman Phil Reid (deceased), Hillary Clinton, and me.

For the 1992 Democratic National Convention, I got together with friends, including Laura Morrison, and members of the Gay & Lesbian Independent Democrats (a Democratic club serving New York County) to make posters (from this silkscreen). We handed them out to LGBT delegates as they entered the convention hall so for the first time ever there would be a visible LGBT presence on the convention floor.

My father came to Dublin with me in 2007, and we marched in that city's St. Patrick's parade (wearing Irish/LGBT stickers). Maybe we'll get to do that one day in the New York City St. Patrick's Day parade!

On a hayride with Kim in New Jersey, 2002.

On vacation in western Canada, summer 2004.

Sadie's first night with us, and she was right at home, 2002.

Meeting President Bill Clinton with my father and sister at the White House Christmas party, December 2000.

Celebrating pride with President Barack Obama at the White House, June 2012, where we spoke with him about the fact that he'd announced support for marriage equality during the week of our wedding. No president has done more for the LGBT community!

Relaxing after a press conference on an East River ferry with Mayor
Michael Bloomberg where we discussed expanded service, 2010.

As Speaker of the City Council, I deliver an annual State of the City Address.
Here I am on February 11, 2013, delivering my final address as Speaker.

March, 10, 2013: Announcing my run for New York City mayor, across the street from Good Shepherd Church, where my parents were married, surrounded by my family, friends, and supporters, including Kim's father, Kim, my father, Ellen, our grand-nephew Jase, and our grand-niece Jordan.

March 10, 2013: the first official day of my campaign for mayor as I kick off a five-borough "Walk and Talk Tour," meeting voters in the Bronx.

With my father on my wedding day, May 19, 2012.

Kim on the arm of her proud father, Anthony Catullo.

Judge Judith Kaye signs our marriage license while our wedding party looks on. *Seated at table, from left to right:* Wayne Kawadler, Judge Judith Kaye, and me. *Standing, from far left to right along the back wall:* Kelley Wisenger, Kevin Catullo, Robert Catullo, Audra Catullo, James Catullo Jr., James Catullo Sr. *Standing, in the middle row behind Wayne Kawadler:* Diane Catullo, Ellen Quinn, Larry Quinn, Anthony Catullo Sr., Dr. Robert Rohrbaugh, Vincent Catullo, John Wisenger, Kim Catullo, Deborah Wisenger. *Standing behind Kim, but not visible:* Terri Catullo.

I've met my match! Dancing at the wedding reception with my friend and anti-gun violence advocate Jackie Rowe-Adams.

Just married! I'd never been happier in my life, and I think it shows.

together chatting. It's the kind of domestic scene I never could have imagined for myself.

Three or four months after buying commitment rings, Kim and I adopted a dog. Looking back, I can see that it further cemented our relationship.

When I met her, I already had Andy, who I'd adopted with my friend and neighbor Wayne. He and I live across the street from each other and had decided to share a dog. We went to the ASPCA. When you walked by the cages, all the dogs came to the front and barked as if they were saying, *Adopt me! Adopt me!* But we decided to sit on the floor near a cage with an open door and wait for a dog named Andy to come out to meet us.

He was much more timid than the other dogs. He was full grown, about eleven months, maybe fifty pounds. He was a shepherd mix with Rottweiler-Doberman coloring and a big shepherd tail that was too big for the rest of his body. He was goofy and cute and irresistible. We asked the ASPCA, "Can we take him out and see if he likes us?" And they said, "Sure," and opened the cage door. But Andy stayed in the back of his cage looking terrified.

We sat there a long time, while he put a paw out and then pulled it back, put the other one out and pulled it back, over and over. He had a horrible background story: he and his siblings had been thrown out the window of a moving car on the Brooklyn-Queens Expressway. So it made sense that he was afraid. After what felt like an hour, he worked up the nerve and stepped out to meet us. It just seemed like he needed somebody to wait for him to come out of the cage. But once he was out, we knew that we wanted to take care of him. The fact that Wayne and I lived across the street from each other made a coparenting arrangement possible; and sharing him made it easier for us to own a dog, because it's a lot of work for just one person.

Kim loved Andy from the first, but Andy was scared of everything. He was okay going outside when we were at the beach, but he didn't like city noise, so we had to drag him outside when we were in Manhattan, which was most of the time. We bought CDs of street noise and played them in the house so he could get used to life in the city.

So Kim and I decided to get another dog. As with Andy, our plan was to share parenting with Wayne.

Kim and I went to North Shore Animal League, intending to get a grown dog because we thought that would be easier. But then we saw Sadie, a puppy. She was in the big-dog section because she was a bit sick and needed to be kept away from the other puppies. She was the one. She's part Shar-Pei and part Lab, so she has excess skin (and had even more as a puppy). She looked so sad and pathetic, curled up in the corner of this huge cage, and so cute with her skin all scrunched up, that we couldn't resist.

Early on, before Kim and I started living together full time, coordinating the dogs was a little complicated, but within a few months I moved into her apartment on Fifth

Avenue in the Village (which was still in my City Council district). Then we moved to my place in London Terrace, a comfortable one-bedroom apartment that was perfect for the two of us and for Andy and Sadie. The big challenge, at least at first, was that Kim is much more organized than I am. When Kim lived alone, she had everything in its place, and that's where it stayed. And that's just not at all what I'm like. There's sense to my order, but it's not the classic sense of order. Over time I think I've helped Kim get less organized, and she'd probably say she's made me less unorganized.

We fell into an easy routine. It helped that we both had demanding jobs, so the fact that I often had commitments outside regular work hours wasn't a problem. But we worried about each other, and we still do. Kim worries about things that go wrong with my work and how they're covered in the press. In politics there's a lot you can't control, and things can easily go wrong, and then you have to read about them in the newspaper. That's one place where we both worry, but despite how upset Kim might feel on my behalf, she works hard at helping me keep things in perspective. That's good because being Irish, I have a tendency to see everything that goes wrong as the end of the world.

It seems that I have not totally gotten over the sense that when things are going bad, it's my fault and mine alone. I'm working on it, but even as an adult, I sometimes feel that everything hinges on me doing everything right. Beyond right—perfectly. So when something doesn't go right, even something simple and insignificant, I can wind up beating myself up. I think it's a residual effect of my mom being sick when I was a kid. If I had a choice, I'd rather not have these feelings. But since I don't have a choice, I have come to believe that it makes me a more focused and thoughtful person. At least I hope so.

Kim helps me understand that not everything is my fault or responsibility. Over the dozen years we've been together, I've come to trust that she often has a better sense than I do of what matters and what doesn't. She's not the kind of person who would ever say, "Oh, it doesn't matter," because she definitely doesn't feel that way. She's very serious about her own work, and when things go wrong, it matters to both of us, but she's really good at keeping things in perspective and taking the long view and saying, "If it doesn't work out, we'll do whatever we want to do."

By that she means that no matter what happens in our work life, we'll still have our life together. Sometimes she jokes about wanting to buy a goat farm in Vermont and make cheese, or at least I take it to be a joke. It had better be a joke. Because as difficult as politics can be, and as hard as I can be on myself, there's no way I'm working on a farm.

CHAPTER 11

Madam Speaker

In 2004 I decided to run for Speaker of the City Council, which is the second-most-powerful elected position in New York City, after mayor. When I look back at my career up to that point, even I'd have to admit that it looks like I'd thoughtfully planned out every step I took, from going to work for Tom Duane, to winning his City Council seat, to getting myself appointed chair of the health committee, to deciding to run for Speaker. But that would give me too much credit. My colleagues know that I'm an insane short-term planner when it comes to plotting out my daily schedule and making sure I'm overprepared. But in a weird way I'm actually not a long-term planner, maybe because I've learned that you never know what might happen around the next corner. I often say that my five-year plan is to be thinner, and that's about it.

Gifford Miller, who was then the Speaker, was running for mayor and couldn't run for City Council again. So the field for Speaker was wide open. I knew I'd be a very long shot. I didn't know if I could win, but there was no value in not trying, because not trying doesn't move you anywhere. Even if I tried and lost, I'd likely be in a better position moving forward. I might get to chair a more influential committee or at least remain health committee chair.

As Speaker you get to work on behalf of the whole city, not just your district and not just whatever's within the purview of a committee. You also get a great deal of input into the citywide legislative agenda. I'd watched Speaker Miller and Mayor Bloomberg deadlock over any number of issues. If either one had compromised, our city would have been better off, I thought. So my goal as Speaker was not to be in a constant battle with the mayor—it was to accomplish things. But first I'd have to get elected.

It was not a simple matter, of course. People were not shy about telling me that I had no chance of winning. They pointed out the obvious: I am from the West Side of Manhattan—a liberal, a woman, and a lesbian. I was fully aware of all these characteristics when I woke up every morning. At some point in the process, I made an important decision: I decided not to listen to them—"the movers and the drainers," as my friend Christine calls them. These self-appointed experts don't help you; in fact, their goal is to hold you back because they don't have the guts to do what you're trying to do. I decided to take another tack, taking a cue from a woman on my staff, who puts it perfectly. It doesn't really matter what the size of the obstacle is, she says; what matters is the angle and speed with which you run to get over it. So I decided to ignore the external and internal naysayers, because sometimes you can be your own worst enemy. I decided to let the people who have a vote in the process speak for themselves.

I wasn't figuring this out all by myself. Running for office is always a team effort. Besides Kim, I had a small and strong group of people working with me and helping me strategize. The race for Speaker is different from other races. It's old school. On the face of it, the Speaker is elected by the fifty other members of the City Council. But in reality, the Democratic county leaders have a huge influence on the process.

In New York City, there are five Democratic Party county leaders, one from each of the city's boroughs: Queens, Brooklyn, the Bronx, Manhattan, and Staten Island. (Each borough is also a county, which is why each has its own party county leader.) Every member of the City Council and every county Democratic leader has an interest in who becomes the Speaker.

There were two basic ways to go about building the support I needed to win. One was to go from the ground up and persuade enough individual members that I was not only the right person for the job but the candidate with the best chance of winning; no one likes to back a loser, and those who back the winner are more likely to have the ear of the new Speaker. The other way is to go from the top down and persuade the Democratic Party county leaders that you're the candidate they should support, and then they in turn encourage their City Council delegation to vote for you.

With five other City Council members in the race, we decided to run a hybrid campaign and work it both ways. Working from the top down meant persuading Democratic county leaders that I would work with them on the issues important to them, and that they could trust me to make the difficult decisions. They needed to be convinced that I would be a strong enough leader to run the City Council and work with the mayor.

Working from the bottom up meant winning over key members of the City Council, as well as key candidates for City Council who, once in office, would vote for me and advocate with county leaders. I also worked on building support with prominent labor leaders and other power brokers in the city who could influence both the City Council members and the Democratic county leaders. It was retail politics with an electorate of several dozen people, and it took more than a year. We all worked like dogs.

In the end, a lot came down to the Queens County Democratic leader, Tom Manton, who wielded the most power of all the Democratic county leaders. The Queens delegation of City Council members, which is the second largest after

Brooklyn, always votes for Speaker as a bloc. And they vote as a bloc with their county leader. It is a brilliant strategy—it increases their power in selecting the Speaker.

The Queens County Democratic Party holds its events at Antun's catering hall. Tom Manton used to hang out there at all of the parties and events. I'd be the first one there and the last to leave, which is my philosophy of work. I believe that you should be the most prepared person in the room, and the first to arrive and the last to leave. People would say, "Oh my god, you're at Antun's for hours! What hard work!" But for me it actually wasn't hard work at all.

I loved listening to Tom and the guys he worked with. His stories of being a cop, his stories of being a councilmember and then a congressman—they were just great. They were colorful, and they were New York. I reveled in it. Queens County and its events were fun. Tom liked ice cream. He would have an ice-cream cart at the events, and he liked people to eat ice cream. He would have a centerpiece on every table. For Christmas there'd be poinsettias, and in the fall there'd be pumpkins. And he urged people to take the centerpieces home—it seemed to make him happy when they took the pumpkins and the poinsettias.

He had great characters surrounding him—Jerry Sweeney, Mike Reich, and Frank Bolz, who we refer to as "the guys." If I said to somebody on my staff, "Call the guys and find out what's going on," everybody would know exactly who I meant. And we had a mother-daughter duo, Mary Lu and Jamie Plunkett. A Plunkett has been on staff at county for fifty years. Everyone, including me, would tell the same story at Queens dinners over and over, but every time you hear it is like the first time.

Queens was pivotal to the Speaker's race, and when I got a call in late 2005 to meet with Tom Manton at his office in Queens, it seemed pretty clear, from everything we were hearing, that I was going to get Tom's support. Tom was the son of Irish immigrants, a seven-term congressman, and a former member of the City Council. He had been on the council in 1986 when they voted on the gay rights bill. The story goes that he had promised everyone he was going to vote for the bill. Then on the day the council voted, Tom's priest brought Tom's father and sat him in the front row, and he voted no.

It would have been easy to tag Tom as antigay from that vote, but his views were more complicated than that, and I suspect it always wore on him that he had not done the right thing. As the Queens County Democratic leader, he was forward-looking. Sometimes political leaders hold on to the ethnic power structure they inherit—whether it's Irish, or Italian, or Jewish, or whatever—and they fight to keep things from changing. Tom didn't see Queens that way. He saw his borough as this open gateway for immigrants, and he saw his county as evolving, and he wanted his political organization to reflect that change. No one ever had to demand it; he just did it. He knew it was right. So when South Asians became a significant part of the population, he appointed a South Asian district leader. The same thing happened with Latinos and later with LGBT people. This was a very big thing for someone who had voted against the gay rights bill.

When I was called to Queens to meet with Tom at his law office, they asked me to come alone. Even though I was pretty sure of what was going to happen, I was still nervous because I didn't know what the conversation was going to be and I'd never been to such a meeting before. What were they going to say they wanted? What kinds of commitments were they going to be looking for? What if what we'd been hearing about Tom's intention to support me was wrong?

When I walked in, Tom was seated at the head of a rectangular table in a classic, nondescript, windowless conference room. Some of "the guys" were sitting around the table.

It turned out that I had nothing to be nervous about, because Tom had already made up his mind. He wanted me for the job. I've since been told I had him at hello. His support and the votes of the Queens delegation were a huge boon to my effort. People will tell you that there are scenarios in which a Speaker wins without Queens, and on paper that's true, but in reality it's impossible.

When the meeting ended, I stood up and walked to the end of the table where Tom was sitting. Normally I called Tom "Congressman," but for some reason on this occasion I said, "Tom, I just want to thank you so much for what you've done for me and my family." I was thanking him for endorsing me and thereby giving me the opportunity to become Speaker. I still had to lock it down, but now it was mine to lose.

In response Tom said, "You're very welcome, but will you grant me absolution?"

I was a bit taken aback, but thinking back to Tom's vote against the gay rights bill, I knew exactly what he meant. So I said, "Tom, I don't need to grant you absolution, but if you grant *me* absolution, I'll grant you absolution, and together we'll go and make this city a much better place."

That's why it's important not to listen to the naysayers. If I had listened to them or to my own naysayer voice, I wouldn't be Speaker, and almost as important, Tom Manton wouldn't have gotten to say what he needed to say or had the opportunity to make it right. Tom died the following summer.

A lot of people were surprised by Tom's endorsement because we often expect others to act based on what they've done in the past. And we don't give people enough credit for their capacity to evolve. Did Tom give me his support because he was attempting to make amends for having voted against the gay rights bill? Or because of our shared Irish heritage? Or because we were similar in a lot of other ways? Was it because he knew how hard I would work? Or all of the above? I'll never know for sure, but I can tell you that when Tom came to my swearing-in at City Hall in January 2006, just a few months before he died, at the conclusion of the swearing-in, he jumped to his feet to applaud before anyone else.

Now it was time to get to work. I had had plenty of op-portunities to watch Gifford Miller do his job as Speaker. I had a clear understanding of the responsibilities and had filed away important lessons that I'd learned from observing, but the new job involved a different order of demands and decisions from what I was accustomed to. It wasn't just that I went from having a staff of six to a staff of three hundred. Or that I was now responsible for deciding who on that staff stayed and who had to go and who served on which commit-tees and who got which committee chair assignments. It was all of that, in combination with stepping onto a fast-moving conveyor belt that didn't stop for anyone. Remember that *I Love Lucy* episode when she works on the conveyor belt boxing chocolates? That's how I felt.

The city runs on an annual calendar, and when I took office in January 2006, I had no choice but to jump in, hang on, and get up to speed as fast as I could. For a self-described perfectionist, this was a prescription for very long days and too many sleepless nights. But I wasn't about to complain.

Well before my swearing-in as the first female and first gay Speaker of the City Council, I knew what kind of Speaker I intended to be. My bottom-line belief in govern-ment is that it should be responsive to the needs of *all* of the people, which meant that as Speaker of the New York City Council, I represented the interests of all New Yorkers in all five boroughs, from small business owners in Brooklyn and the elderly rent-controlled tenant in the Bronx to the owner of the brokerage house on Wall Street, the homeowner in Queens, the car service driver on Staten Island, and the housing authority residents on the Lower East Side.

Sometimes the energy to make changes comes from the people you know, people whose relationships and stories are often indelible. Take, for example, my friend Jackie Adams, who lost two sons to gun violence. One died in Baltimore, and the other in Harlem. She had asked her son to go to the deli to get milk, and he never came home. I love her. This woman has formed a group called Harlem Mothers Save. They meet every Wednesday night in Harlem, and it's a support group for mothers who've lost kids to gun violence. In the face of this loss, she's the most positive woman you'll ever meet in your life. She is fighting for her community.

Early in my term as Speaker, Harlem was suffering from a plague of gang-initiated graffiti, which included an image of a rat holding up a sign that said "Stop Snitching." Jackie called and asked if she could see me. I said, "Sure, sure." And she came to the office and sat down in a big governmental club chair that swallowed her tiny self up. She told me about the "Stop Snitching" signs, and we decided we had to do something. We went with other mothers and painted over all the graffiti. But what touched me was when she asked, "Can I tell the women on Wednesday that you're with us?"

I said, "Sure."

She started to cry.

"Why are you crying?" I asked.

"You don't understand," she said. "You're the Speaker of the City Council."

This conversation brought home to me the significance of my job to regular New Yorkers.

In a job like mine, getting things done is essential, even if it means compromising on an issue to move things forward. No one elected me to just say no. Deadlock is not a formula for government. In the past, I'd had a ringside seat when things would grind to a halt because the council and the mayor had frequently locked horns and wouldn't compromise. I made a conscious decision to do it differently, to work with the mayor, because spitting at each other and wagging fingers isn't governing. I saw Mayor Bloomberg as my colleague. If I was going to be an effective Speaker and we were going to move forward on an agenda that made things better for New Yorkers, I needed him, and he needed me.

That seems like an old-fashioned way of thinking, in these times where standoffs are the rule. And some people have criticized me for working so well with the mayor. But I never doubted that he and I could work together. We already had a track record of working together respectfully even when we didn't agree. He and I worked *with* each other on the smoking ban, and we worked *against* each other when he was pushing a plan to build a football stadium on Manhattan's West Side—in my district. The project was critically important for the mayor because of his aspirations to bring the Olympics to New York. But I thought it would be terrible for my district and a bad thing for the city overall. I did everything I could to get that project killed. But later he and I worked together on rezoning the proposed stadium site for new office and residential development. He certainly didn't like that I had helped kill his stadium proposal, but we both knew that we would live to see another day—to agree or disagree, then move on to the next issue.

I believe that my drive to get as much done as possible goes back to my experience of my mother dying young. Because the idea "I'll get another opportunity" just doesn't exist in my way of looking at things. That might seem morbid, but it's quite effective: every moment could be your last, so you have to try to make the most of it. So the idea that I would become Speaker and then squander it for the sake of press or politics or whatever, as opposed to just getting as much done as possible, is unimaginable to me because it's completely counter to the reality that life is incredibly short.

Working with Mayor Bloomberg and his office was a pleasure after Rudy Giuliani, who had been mayor when I first came to the City Council and whose administration Tom Duane had fought with. Back then Tom and I had been trying to get somebody who lived in a housing project a new toilet, and the manager had said, "You'll have to call the mayor's office." I was like, "Really?" And the manager said, "Yes, everything is going through City Hall."

So I called City Hall, and they said, "That's right, we're taking all constituent issues."

And I said, "You guys, that's impossible! I mean, how are you possibly going to take all of this in?" Handling it all through City Hall was not only controlling but ineffective.

Once, when I was on the council during Mayor Giuliani's term, I was meeting with a commissioner, and the commissioner's secretary came in and said, "Deputy Mayor so-and-so is on the way."

"Okay, I'll wrap up," I said.

"Wrap up? You'll get out!" the commissioner said.

"What are you talking about?"

"We're not allowed to meet with you," he explained. "I didn't get this meeting approved by City Hall."

And so my chief of staff and I had to go out through the loading dock of that building. Literally, we climbed over boxes to get out, and this commissioner was frantic that a deputy mayor might see me.

Criticism of me as Speaker went into high gear in 2008, when Mayor Bloomberg proposed extending term limits so he could run for a third term. I had to decide whether to support his proposal. The choice wasn't at all clear, and I struggled to balance what was best for him, for the city, for the City Council, and for me personally. (Extending term limits would affect me, too, because it would likely mean putting off plans to run for mayor and serving another four years on the City Council.) We were in a truly tough moment in the city. The bottom had just fallen out of the economy, and we were bracing for the worst recession since the Depression.

Deciding whether to support Mayor Bloomberg on term limits was further complicated by the fact that voters had twice approved limiting the city's elected officials to two four-year terms. Going against the majority of voters on any issue is never easy. Before the mayor proposed the change, I'd made it clear that the voters had spoken and that I would not support a change in the law. I also had to consider what I'd said in the past about term limits, and whether I wanted to change my position. But now that Mayor Bloomberg had proposed just such a change, I felt compelled in my role as Speaker to consider the many, often contentious voices. And I felt compelled to hold my tongue and keep my thoughts to myself, as people on both sides of the issue made their views known in the press, via e-mail, on the street, and in the corridors of City Hall.

Before I made my decision, I met personally with dozens of councilmembers, who were not at all shy about telling me what they thought, one way or another. I spoke with union leaders and representatives from good-government groups, some of whom supported term limits and some of whom opposed them. My usual goal was to find common ground, but on this issue either you were for or against, because there was no middle ground. My decision to keep my thoughts to myself until the very end and focus on listening to the debate didn't win me any friends in the press or with people on either side of the divide.

Before the City Council took a final vote, we had two

days (and nearly twenty hours) of spirited public hearings to amend the city charter to override the term limits law. I decided to support the mayor and let the voters decide whether to give him a third term. And my constituents, many of whom were furious with me for supporting the mayor, got to decide too. The voters spoke. They reelected the mayor, and they elected me to a third term in the City Council. But neither of us won with huge majorities.

The whole experience with extending term limits was tough, but on reflection I have no regrets about my decision. I think that all too often politicians take a position and never leave themselves open to the possibility that circumstances may change, or that they may learn new information, or that the world may change, and that a position that at one point seemed cast in stone was worth reconsidering. I see no crime in that, and, in fact, I think it's essential.

Nothing takes up more time on the City Council's calendar than the budget. In January the mayor presents his preliminary budget. Then we review the budget and hold hearings—it's a very involved process. The mayor then takes into consideration (or doesn't) what comes out of the hearings and presents his executive budget in May. Between May and the end of June, it's all budget all the time, but the real negotiations don't start until June because you have to have a series of public hearings first. I've always thought it was rude to the public to be engaged in significant negotiations on the budget while the public hearings were still going on, because they're coming to tell us what they think about the budget. And what the public thinks about the budget should in part inform our priorities.

As lead negotiator for the City Council, I'm in constant motion. My life is a steady litany of input and decisions. "This is where we're at." "Do you think we should push on this?" "Should we accept that?" "I need you to think about this." "We're nowhere!" "Go back and try again!" And on and on. My first year was brutal, and not just for me. In addition to specific issues, my staff and I had to deal with all the broader budget issues. Should we raise taxes? If so, what kind? Should we cut this? Does the Department of Transportation need more funding because it was a bad winter and the roads are a mess? Does the Department of Education need more money for this or that? Should we put more dollars into the police? Should we keep all the firehouses open? And what about the specific requests from councilmembers? And what about my own priorities. I lost my temper from time to time negotiating all these issues, but somehow we all got through it, and it got easier each year: not because the decisions were necessarily easier to make, but because I learned how to work with my staff so that they could work with the mayor's staff and we could have more effective and less contentious negotiations. Still, by definition the budget process is not easy and it's messy. And each year's budget presents its own problems because of the specific issues the city faces, and this changes from year to year.

I was quickly reminded that no one in city government, including the Speaker, has absolute power. The mayor proposes the budget, and we negotiate and then adopt. Over the course of negotiating seven budgets, we struggled to keep tax increases to a minimum, and to limit layoffs, and the budget was always balanced. The heartbreak for me was that the financial collapse in 2008 forced us to make painful cuts, but none that I believed would put lives at risk. It's extremely difficult when you don't have enough money to do everything you'd like to do and you're not able to fully fund the social services that you know are good and necessary. It's excruciating to have to tell people, "You're not going to get the amount of money you need to do the work you do."

There have also been wonderful times. Housing is a passion of mine. In a city the size of New York, there are invariably going to be a handful of landlords who let their buildings fall apart. They're interested in collecting rent and don't care about anything else, and they just assume they'll never get caught. So you wind up with buildings where tenants are living in appalling conditions.

The problem was—and had been for a long time—that the city didn't have strong enough laws in place to force these owners to do what needed to be done.

Before I became Speaker, given my history as a housing organizer, fixing up dilapidated housing was one of my major priorities. So once I became Speaker and was in a position to do something, we drafted and passed the Safe Housing Law. It focuses on the landlords who owned the two hundred worst buildings—the ones that have the most violations. This wasn't just a matter of peeling paint and broken faucets. I remember visiting one building in Brooklyn and it was disgusting. I almost vomited from the garbage and the maggots. The conditions were unsafe and inhuman.

To come up with an effective bill, my staff and I worked for a year with both tenant advocates and real estate folks, all in the room together. You couldn't do it without the landlords, because they know how the buildings work. They're not interested in protecting the slumlords, but they're also not interested in letting all landlords get painted with a broad brush. We went about writing the bill with the recognition that not every building in the city of New York needs a big hammer, or that much attention, but that we should be targeting the worst buildings with greater attention.

Everybody said there was no way we could come up with a meaningful bill that all sides would support, but we did. The bill gave the Department of Housing's code-enforcement unit more latitude to arrange the necessary repairs on these buildings, and it gave the city the ability to sue these landlords and seize their assets to pay for the work that the city had done. And at the end of the day, if a landlord didn't pony up and fix things, we could take away the building and sell it to a responsible nonprofit or to the tenants or to some other entity that would manage and maintain it properly.

The bill passed and was signed into law. We held a press conference at a building in Brooklyn that was in really bad condition but was about to enter the new program as the first building to fall under our new law. A few months later we went back to see the building after it was redone, and it really looked nice.

We visited another building about ten blocks away that was a horror show, and we were able to tell the people there that we'd done something that would help them. I could see skepticism in their eyes, and I didn't blame them, because I could only imagine how many times their government had said it'd do something to help them and then nothing had happened. But I was able to say, "Don't believe me. Go see what the city did to your neighbors' building. This community organizer can take you there." And they went. Knowing that their building would get to be as livable as the other one because of the Safe Housing Law was just a remarkable feeling.

My only disappointment was that I wanted to do that press conference in Brooklyn with everybody—with both tenant organizers and landlords. But they refused to stand at a press conference with each other! I learned a long time ago that you never get everything you want, and this was one of those occasions where I had to be satisfied that I got nearly everything. And now we have a powerful weapon in the fight against deadbeat landlords.

PART III

The Circle of Joy and Sorrow

CHAPTER 12

A Day in the Life

The pace of social change sometimes moves at warp speed, yet sometimes it's hard to remember what things were like before the change occurred. For many of us, marriage equality is an example of the acceleration of events. It seems so obvious to us now, and public opinion across the country has changed radically. But it doesn't take a feat of memory to recall the time before everything changed.

There was never a question in my mind that I would take an active role in lobbying state officials to vote in favor of granting same-sex couples the legal right to marry, because first and foremost I believed that passing marriage equality in New York was the right thing to do. Here's why: if you have part of a law that affirmatively *excludes* a group of people—that says one group of people is less significant than another, and that it's okay for that group to be left out of the framework of society—then it's not only bad for that group, it sends the message to the larger society that it's okay to have second-class citizens. But beyond that, it's a kind of cancer on the law books, because if a law can affirmatively set aside the rights of one group of people, what's going to stop discrimination from spreading to other groups that are out of favor with the larger society?

As long as marriage is available, it should be available to everyone and anyone who wants it. It's very important for the state to make certain that each family knows that it is recognized and supported and taken into consideration in the same way as every other family. The laws of the State of New York have to reach their arms out and wrap themselves around people in order to change a discriminatory policy into a legal affirmation. And for the State of New York to do this would send an affirmative message that it is a jurisdiction that is inclusive of everyone. That would have a ripple effect across the country. And that's extremely important from both a political and a societal perspective.

At a personal level, I see legal marriage as the way we in society affirm relationships. You could ask, "Shouldn't relationships be a private thing?" But the truth is that some events are so significant that society has to witness and affirm them in order to really recognize them, whether it's the swearing-in of the president of the United States or a marriage ceremony. That was something I thought LGBT people deserved and was going to be a powerfully good thing for people and families.

Once the formal effort to pass marriage equality legislation in New York got under way in 2008, I felt compelled to participate for reasons beyond the fact that it was the right thing to do. First, before I was elected Speaker, I believed it was my responsibility, as one of the few openly LGBT members of the City Council, to represent the interests of all LGBT people in New York City. Each LGBT elected official out there feels that responsibility to a different degree; I believed it strongly. And I don't think it's any different for any other elected officials: You have your geographic constituency, which is based on the boundaries of the physical area you represent. And then you have a constituency based on who you are, to which you may feel a particular responsibility—to take a leading role on women's issues or Irish issues or LBGT issues or African American issues or Latino issues or wherever you feel your particular voice can have a positive impact in representing the interests of your constituents.

Also, as the highest-ranking LGBT elected official in the city, it was part of my broader job description to get directly involved in lobbying for the marriage equality bill by meeting with the state senators who held the keys to the bill's passage. (By this point it was clear that the state assembly and the governor were on board and that only the senate was standing in the way.) And as Speaker, just by showing up I would be sending a far more powerful message to the senators than I could have as an elected official from Greenwich Village: the message that this was important legislation for the City of New York and, not incidentally, important to me personally. And as a gay woman who was partnered and wanted to be legally married, I could use my personal story in a way that I hoped would be persuasive with senators who needed persuading. For a lot of these senators, our meeting would be the first time they'd had to engage a high-ranking gay official, one who contradicted their perception that being LGBT was a negative, at least in terms of running for higher office.

In some ways the fight for marriage equality was the end point of a two-decade effort to get domestic partnership recognition and benefits for same-sex couples. Years before marriage equality was even on the radar, when I was still a tenant organizer, I was involved in helping couples with basic issues, like protecting housing rights. New York is a city of renters, and quite often for gay and lesbian couples, only one partner's name is on the lease. So if that partner dies—and huge numbers of gay men were dying in the 1980s through the mid-1990s—the surviving partner had no succession rights and could be evicted.

When I began my job for ANHD in 1989, a case working its way through the appeals process—*Braschi v. Stahl*—involved a gay man, Miguel Braschi, whose long-term partner had died. He was being evicted from the rent-controlled apartment they'd lived in together for more than a decade. (New York City has different kinds of rent regulations, the strictest being laws that were put in place during World War II to keep rents from spiking during a time when housing was in short supply.) In 1989, New York City's rent regulations stated that upon the death of a rent-protected tenant, the landlord might not dispossess "either the surviving spouse of the deceased tenant or some other member of the deceased tenant's family who has been living with the tenant."

In *Braschi v. Stahl,* the lower court decided against Braschi because it didn't consider him a spouse or a family member. One of the things I did was organize people to go to court to be there to watch the proceedings. Tom Duane, who was superinvolved in the case, told me about a press conference he organized where a Chelsea neighborhood activist said, "Before the body was cold, the landlord was evicting him!" The appeals court decided in favor of Braschi, which meant that nontraditional partners or domestic partners, whether their names were on the lease or not, had to be recognized for the purposes of succession rights—effectively adding them to the automatic succession rights of "other family members."

It was a huge win, both because so many people's homes were no longer at risk and because the decision set a precedent for other cases involving domestic partners. It opened the door to a push for other domestic partner rights, from health benefits to civil unions and eventually to marriage itself. For me personally, that case was significant because it was the first time I could put my finger on why legal recognition of same-sex couples was an imperative, whether or not you were in favor of marriage.

Once I was on the City Council, during the years before I became Speaker, the big push at the city level was for an equal benefits bill, which was modeled after a San Francisco law that required entities that had contracts with the city to provide domestic partnership benefits. The point of that bill—for which I was the lead sponsor—was to get benefits for domestic partners; but even more important, it would demonstrate that we in city government had pushed the envelope as far as we could in recognizing gay families. We did everything to support the bill, from lobbying members of the City Council and community organizing to organizing businesses. The council passed the bill, but Mayor Bloomberg vetoed it. The council overrode the veto. The mayor's office brought a lawsuit claiming that passage of the bill was a violation of the City Council's powers, because we don't have power over contracts, which is actually true. Mayor Bloomberg didn't disagree with the content of the bill, but he thought the City Council had overstepped its legislative authority. We had tried to be creative about how we wrote the legislation, doing it in a way that threaded the needle, but the court didn't agree, and we lost. It was a big defeat.

When marriage equality finally became a legislative

possibility in New York in 2009, a coalition of statewide gay rights groups led the organizing, with a focus on the state senate. I looked to these organizations to tell me who were the potential or likely yes votes. Sometimes they would reach out to me and tell me who needed to be lobbied, and sometimes we'd go to them and ask, "How can we help? What more do you need from us?" Tons of people worked tirelessly on trying to get the bill passed, but frankly, in retrospect, it was something of a seat-of-the-pants effort, and when the vote came on December 2, 2009, we lost in a landslide—38 to 24. Despite the support of then governor David Paterson, Mayor Michael Bloomberg, and the Senate Democratic leadership, all thirty Republican senators voted against the bill, along with eight Democrats. The loss stung, and I took it personally.

At a press conference two days later, I was angry and upset. When the last questioner asked what I thought happened, I said:

> *I think we lost is what happened. What's important now is to figure out what we do moving forward. There are lots of factors that we can all hypothesize about. Could all of us have done more? Everyone can always do more. But at the end of the day, people did the wrong thing [by voting against marriage equality]. There may, in fact, be a lot of very abstract, fair political outside factors that made this vote very dif-*

ficult for people. But I don't care. You know . . . my father is eighty-three years old. Kim's father is eighty-three years old. Our mothers died when we were girls, coincidentally. Mine when I was sixteen, Kim's when she was seventeen. So how a roomful of people who've never met me don't think it's fair to [increase] the likelihood that her father and my father can see us dance at our wedding . . . Well, I don't really care about a coup [by conservatives in the state legislature]. I don't care that people ganged up on Dede Scozzafava, who's a courageous woman. What I care about is that my life isn't any better today.

Dede, a Republican state assemblywoman, was stripped of her Republican leadership position for voting in favor of the marriage equality bill.

The next morning Kim and I were having breakfast at Moonstruck, our neighborhood diner, and were both feeling down. One of the waiters, who must have seen a news clip from the press conference, stopped at our table and said, "Don't worry—your fathers will live to walk you down the aisle." It was sweet of him to say, but given New York State politics, the chances of a new marriage equality bill coming up for a vote anytime soon—let alone getting approved by the state senate after being defeated by such a large margin—were slim to none. And our fathers weren't getting any younger.

But it turns out the waiter knew more than I did. Andrew

Cuomo, who was elected governor a year later, cared deeply about marriage equality. Early on he said he would define success in his first year by whether he accomplished three things: fixing the state budget, passing new ethics legislation, and signing marriage equality into law. He made clear that he thought New York was losing its identity as the Empire State, in part because it was no longer a leader in human rights.

New York has such a history of human and civil rights leadership. It was a birthplace of the women's suffrage movement, the women's rights movement, in 1848, and a major stop on the Underground Railroad. It passed the first equal employment laws in the postwar era. And in 1969 the uprising at Stonewall, right in our city, signaled a new push for gay rights. Governor Cuomo believed that the state legislature's defeat of marriage equality was a blot on the state's record. To be seen as a leader again, New York couldn't leave behind a portion of our citizens.

This second time around was totally different. After we'd lost the first time, people did a brutal and honest debrief and came up with a much more orderly plan for how to persuade enough senators to vote yes. Governor Cuomo and his people essentially chaired the enterprise, which made the difference. Over the course of the two lobbying campaigns—first in 2009, and then again in 2011, I probably had two dozen or so formal meetings with state senators, mostly in Albany, and in addition I hung around the halls of the state capitol, where people I needed to talk to wandered in and out. I'd wave and maybe walk with them from one part of the capitol to another, maybe follow them until I could get a moment with them. It was like what I did in college, lobbying at the Connecticut state capitol.

The legislators gave me a whole range of responses. Some were pleasant, even if they weren't going to be with me in the final vote. Others were strikingly personal and serious and deliberate in their thinking. Some were, out of nowhere, oddly honest. Many were appropriately concerned about the impact their vote would have on their district and on their prospects for being reelected.

The vote in Albany was to be held the week of June 20. The timing made my life a little bit complicated, because a month or two earlier our niece Kelley had asked to have her college graduation party at our beach house. I'd suggested Saturday, June 25, the day before the LGBT Pride Parade. After the party, we'd have to head back to the city Saturday night or Sunday morning to march in the parade, but it was no big deal. Kim's immediate response was "Are you crazy?" She had a point—which I dutifully disregarded.

It was also budget time, and though I believed we would finish negotiating early, there was no guarantee—you never knew what would happen, or when. Kim said we should find another date for the party, but I insisted, "No, the budget is going to be over early. I know it. We'll be able to run up to Albany to watch the vote, and I'm going to take that Friday off to prepare for the party. We'll get it all done, and you don't have to worry. It'll be fine."

Those were dangerous words. What I didn't count on was that the budget negotiations would drag on, in large part because I was determined to avoid laying off four thousand teachers. Still, at the start of the week, I was hopeful that I could wrap up the negotiations in time to go to Albany and then take Friday off. I'd packed a bag and kept it at my office. At the beginning of every budget meeting, I'd ask, "What's the Albany update?"—some people in those meetings were also monitoring what was going on at the capitol. But by the end of the day on Wednesday, I'd given up hope of seeing the vote. We were still working out the final budget details. Of course everything wound up coming to a head on Friday— the last day possible for both the budget and the Albany vote. The LGBT Pride Parade was Sunday, so if the vote didn't happen, we were going to have a disaster on our hands.

The budget negotiations were going down to the line. We were in a financial crunch, and the mayor was right that we needed to cut money from the budget. But he proposed that we lay off four thousand teachers, which was not right. I knew it was bad for the city and terrible for our children. The mayor and his people were immovable on the four thousand teachers unless they got some concessions. But I just kept saying to him, "We're not going to do this."

And I kept saying to the unions, "I don't want to do this, but I need help, because I don't have enough money to prevent this from happening."

Finally the unions asked, "Well, what do you want us to do?"

I told them the truth. "I don't have any idea what I want you to do, but you know your contracts better than I do. You don't like the concessions the mayor's proposed, so propose your own. Because this is not going to work, I don't have that much money."

I said the same thing over and over to everyone: "I need your help. I need your help. I need your help. I need your help."

Harry Nespoli, the head of the municipal labor committee, came up with a proposal that would have prevented layoffs across the board for all unions; it wasn't acceptable to the mayor, so we reworked it to another proposal. The majority of the unions rejected that, but in this kind of process, continuing to ask, and refusing to take no for an answer from anybody, can actually work.

Finally, the UFT, the teachers' union, came up with $80 million worth of concessions. We needed $270 million, but that concession changed the whole dynamic—we were able to get the mayor to help us come up with the rest of the money and save the jobs. I had invoked my old strategy: I wouldn't stop asking for help, and I wouldn't give up. I just was not willing to settle for no. And it was funny; it wasn't until the day when the clock was literally going to run out that we were able to get a deal. That morning I still didn't know if we were going to be able to get a deal.

It was a nerve-racking morning. At City Hall, we had the down-to-the-wire budget negotiations with four thousand teachers' jobs on the line, and in Albany we had marriage equality hanging by a thread. Nothing was working on either issue. I left City Hall and raced across the street to the office building at 250 Broadway. I kept saying to the staff, "Call the union back. Call the mayor's people back. Make them keep talking. We have to keep talking." And somehow we just got there. The second we had an agreement, we just said, "Get the councilmembers in here—we've got to get this done now." It wasn't ultimately a hard sell, but we still had a lot of people to talk to.

In a perfect world, we would have wrapped up the budget deal early enough on Friday to do our ceremonial handshake at City Hall live for the six o'clock news. (In government lingo, the big press conference where you announce you have a budget deal is called the "handshake," because after you announce the budget deal, the mayor and the Speaker step in front of the podium and shake hands, and the mayor and I kiss. The kissing part is probably a recent addition.) But the deal came together so late that we missed the six o'clock news. So we decided to schedule it for ten p.m. We figured that by then the vote in Albany would have happened.

Kim had gone to the beach house on the Jersey shore, to get ready for the party. Throughout the day I'd kept her posted on what I was hearing from Albany—the senate Republicans had had a marathon nine-hour debate that day just on whether to allow the bill to come to the floor of the full senate. But they finally allowed it.

Toward the end of the day, I told her I thought the vote would come that night and that we were going to win. Her response was a blunt "Yeah, right."

"No, I mean it," I said. "It all really comes down to Senator Saland."

Before the final vote, the senate had to vote on an amendment regarding religious exemptions, and if Senator Stephen Saland voted in favor of it, which seemed likely since he'd crafted the language, the handful of other courageous Republicans who indicated they might (or would) vote in favor of the final bill would likely ultimately do so.

Kim and I were on the phone while we watched that first vote together, and once Senator Saland voted for the amendment, I said, "It's going to happen now."

Kim said, "Chris, I'm not going to get excited."

"It's going to happen," I said, because at that point we were so close.

She wasn't convinced. "I'm not going to believe it until it actually happens."

After Senator Saland voted, I headed over to the Tweed Courthouse for our budget press conference. Because the big budget issue had been the massive teacher layoffs, and we'd avoided them, we decided to hold the press conference at that courthouse, which is where the Department of Education's headquarters are located. We knew the final vote on the marriage equality bill in Albany would happen during our handshake, so we set up a system with the mayor's press secretary to give us the high sign when it passed. We wanted to deliver news of the vote as soon as it came in. The plan was to adjourn the budget press conference, and the mayor and I would each make a statement on marriage equality.

During the press conference, Meghan Linehan, my deputy chief of staff, walked into the room through a side door and jumped up and down with a huge smile on her beaming face.

I touched the mayor on his shoulder. "I think the bill has passed."

So the mayor said, "We have great news from Albany."

We wrapped up the budget and moved on to marriage equality. The TV cameras got what I said on tape.

> *It's hard to describe the feeling of having the law of your state change to say that what you know in your heart is true, that you are a full member of the state and that your family is as good as any other family. Tomorrow, my family will gather for my niece's college graduation party and that'll be a totally different day because we'll get to talk about when our wedding will be and what it'll look like and what dress Jordan, our grandniece, will wear as the flower girl. And that's a moment I really thought would never come.*

As much as I said I was sure this bill would pass, I was never sure this bill would pass. And even this morning as I said to my partner while getting ready for the day, I was so nervous because I had begun to plan the wedding in my mind and I thought, What if it doesn't happen again? The disappointment will be so tremendous. And the feeling now is so overwhelming. To see Senator Saland stand up there and talk about the journey he had gone through to get to this point. To see senators stand up and overcome their fear of what the voters will do to them or they fear the voters will do in the voting booth—it's an amazing day.

And what it does for me is important, but what it does for gay children is indescribable. There are children who are watching this vote right now across the country in households that are free to tell people that they believe that they are gay and they just saw the legislature of the greatest state in the Union say that they are equal and that they matter. That will keep children alive. It will give them hope. And it will tell them that it does get better and that they matter.

What a night! Working together, we had prevented teacher layoffs, and marriage equality had become the law of our state. As soon as I could, I ducked out of the press conference to call Kim. I cried tears of joy—for a change. As I later told a reporter, I slipped out of my James Cagney tough-girl mode. I got down to the shore at about one-thirty a.m., and Kim met me on the porch, and we hugged and were thrilled. But not for long because we had fifty-five people coming that day for Kelley's graduation party, and we had to be up early to prepare.

The party was so much fun. My father came, too, and when I greeted him on the porch, he shook my hand and said, "You've had a productive week, child. Keep it up."

Classic LQ.

Kim and I marched in the LGBT Pride Parade with Governor Cuomo; the mayor; the governor's girlfriend, Sandra Lee; and my father. I'd been to many pride marches and the crowds are always amazing, but this one was emotional in a way that none had ever been. It was only two days after the vote, and the crowds—hundreds of thousands of people packed in on the sidewalks along the entire parade route—were wild with excitement. People were weeping. They were screaming, "Thank you!" "We love you!"

After we reached the end of the parade route, Kim and I walked back so we could do the parade again and march with the Gay and Lesbian Independent Democrats, which is my home Democratic club. I figured the second time wouldn't be as intense because we weren't with the governor or the mayor and we didn't have a big banner, but the response from the crowds was just as wildly happy as the first time around. By the time we got to the end of the parade route for the second time, we were wiped. Kim and I went home and enjoyed a rare quiet night alone together.

We only had a month before the bill went into effect, on Sunday, July 24. Take my word for it, there was a lot to sort out and tons of logistics to put in place, but we got it done. We set up a lottery such that eight hundred couples could get married that first day. By early Sunday morning, July 24, the eight hundred couples were lining up at the city clerk's offices across the city, waiting for the offices to open at nine a.m.

I was at the city clerk's office and walked the line to congratulate the couples as they waited to go inside. As I was shaking everybody's hands, I got to two women, Deirdre Weaver and Nancy Grass, who were all dressed up. Deirdre was clearly a cancer survivor (I learned later that she'd had breast cancer). Her hair was all fuzzy and thin, and you could see it hadn't grown all the way back in yet. I asked her, "How long?" And she figured I was asking how long since her diagnosis. She said, "Eight months." It was an emotional day to begin with, but I was overwhelmed. It made me think about the family members who would be at my wedding and those who would not, and about how here was this woman recovering from cancer, and now her family was getting recognized. This couple's moment summed up the entire reason we had all engaged in the marriage effort.

I went to watch the first couple be married in Manhattan. I remember hearing the city clerk say, "By the power vested in me by the laws of the State of New York, I marry you." But for the first time the clerk was saying it for two women, two elderly women who had been together for more than twenty years. One was in a wheelchair with a neck brace. She got out of her wheelchair with her walker, and the other woman helped her, and it was just so lovely. They were lovely, and they had waited decades, and one of the most moving things about them was that the one who was just as old as the other was helping her stand up. Mike McSweeney, who had been a Tom Manton protégé, was the city clerk, and he got to marry them. I later learned that the woman outside who had breast cancer was his college best friend—she had come down so he could marry her.

And then there were two guys in Brooklyn. When the judge said, "Do you have rings?" they couldn't get their rings off, because they had been wearing them for so long. The judge said, "Let's not break any bones here, guys." In Queens I took pictures of a newly married couple, and all their kids were dressed in white tuxedoes and white dresses. The *Daily News* sponsored a wedding at the Old Homestead. A couple of women won the prize, an all-expenses-paid wedding party. But one of their parents had died recently. It made me realize that the delay from 2009 meant a big difference because some people's family members didn't get to see their weddings.

That day I went to Manhattan, Brooklyn, and Queens, and I ended the day at Gracie Mansion, where the mayor presided over the marriage of his criminal justice coordinator and a commissioner. What a day!

This wonderful day was of course tinged with sadness and loss. I was overwhelmed with joy, but at the same time I remembered all those who weren't with us. We do a disservice to people when, after a bad thing occurs in their lives, we promote the belief that they will one day be wholly free of grief and sadness. The truth is, grief will always be with you. It does not have to be crippling or even a bad thing; it is part of you and your life and your world. At times it will feel uncomfortable or even painful and horrible, and at times it will be useful or even powerful. It will work for you if it enhances your capacity to be empathetic or fuels your desire to make the world a better, safer, and healthier place, or if it helps you seize each day. You just have to let yourself feel the bad stuff and cry your eyes out, then fix your makeup and get on with it.

CHAPTER 13

Light and Shadow

I never expected to get married. That wasn't in the cards
for me—I had given up on that part of life. I enjoyed leafing
through bridal magazines, but only as an observer. My world
changed gradually. First, Kim and I found each other, which
meant that love—deep and abiding love—would be part of
my life's portion. Then the law changed, and holding a wedding in our city, with our friends and our family, was going
to happen. I thought about the waiter at Moonstruck who
comforted us the day after marriage equality lost in Albany
and predicted that our fathers would walk us down the aisle.
How right he was. Kim and I pinched ourselves because it
was still hard to believe that we actually could get married.
Since we had been together so long and had only ten months

to plan our gala wedding, we agreed to skip the formal engagement and get on with arranging it.

Kim had other plans. One evening after we came home from a party, Kim put on a song that we had played constantly when we first met. I guessed she wanted me to consider using it for the wedding or for the rehearsal dinner, and I said, "That's nice."

"Turn off the TV," she said.

"I really want to see this segment." I didn't look away from the screen.

Next she brought out a mug, which was a special gift from one of our early Valentine's Days together—it has a heart and the word *Forever* on it, and it has a lot of meaning for us.

I took the mug from her and said, "Yeah, that's great," and put it down on the coffee table.

Finally Kim said, "Will you turn off the damn TV and look?!?"

I looked inside the mug and found a receipt from Bowlmor Lanes in Greenwich Village, where we had had our second date. I had written my phone number on the back of it. Unbeknownst to me, Kim had kept it all those years.

"Turn it over."

On the other side she'd written, "Will you marry me?"

I don't know if I was laughing or crying at this point or both, but I managed to say, "Of course I'm going to marry you!"

I looked inside the mug again and found a small box and opened it.

"This is your mom's ring, right?"

Kim *loved* her mother. She hadn't given me just any ring—it was her mother's ring, and I knew how much it meant to her. The week after the marriage equality bill passed, she had taken her mother's engagement ring and gone to see our favorite jewelers, the Doyle sisters on the Lower East Side, to get it spruced up. She debated adding emeralds because they're green (me being Irish) or sapphires, the birthstone of the month we met. She decided on sapphires.

The next weekend when Kim's dad visited our house, we told him we wanted to show him something. I held out my hand, and he looked at the ring. "Is that Mom's?" he asked Kim.

She said yes, and he started to cry. Kim's parents had been very much in love. Her father had never remarried after Kim's mom died. Kim's mother was the love of his life.

Over lunch with Kim's sister, Debbie, and her husband and Kim's brother Anthony, Kim's father told us about the ring. He had bought it from a jeweler in Newark for eight hundred dollars, which was a lot of money at the time, and had proposed to Kim's mother under the cherry blossom trees in Branch Brook Park during the annual Cherry Blossom Festival in Newark. That gave us an idea for how to decorate the wedding hall, because our wedding was to be in the spring, right around cherry blossom time.

I had no experience planning a wedding. There hadn't been a Quinn family wedding since my sister got married the September after our mother died, and it had been a small one. The important thing for both of us was that our wedding be personal, that it reflect who we are, and that it not be a political event. The personal issue was key—and that guided us throughout the planning.

For the most part we wanted a traditional ceremony, and for a while we considered including a religious element— we're both Catholic—like having a priest give a blessing at the end. But we were sure the priest would get in trouble and it would wind up in the newspapers. How to deal with the press was something we struggled with. We didn't want to be seen as exploiting the wedding for political reasons, but we also didn't want to seem like we were embarrassed or ashamed and trying to hide anything. It was challenging to find a balance, especially since Kim does *not* do interviews, a policy that she was not going to change for the wedding. In the end we decided to give certain advance information to the press, and we provided photos afterward, but we didn't want any press at the wedding itself. That would have been incredibly intrusive and would have made public something that was very personal to us.

The press got wind of our engagement, and Kim's dad was quoted as saying that I was "a great catch" and that he was "very happy when Kim told me that she and Chris were getting married." He went on, "The whole family got to know Chris well, and we thought the world of her. I knew how much she meant to Kim and that they loved each other very much." My father responded in typical form: "It's nice that [Christine] found a pal to share her life with." Referring to the change in his thinking since I'd first told him I was gay, he said, "There's been an evolution." I was proud of him for the distance he'd come over those years and for saying so to the reporter. Both our fathers were pleased to be able to walk us down the aisle.

After the wedding friends sent us a three-page spread from a newspaper in Norway. Another friend saw something about it in India. Kim's old college roommate from New Jersey, who made the cake (a five-tiered chocolate chip cake with chocolate custard and buttercream frosting), wound up on the local evening news. And in New York it was on the front page of every newspaper. But to us, from beginning to end, it was our wedding, and we did everything we could to make it a personal celebration, from the invitations, the guest list, and the decorations, to the readings and our vows.

I'd figured that planning a wedding would be a lot of work, but it turned out to be an even more humongous job than I imagined. Because of my work, it was almost instantaneously clear that it would be impossible for me to take the lead. Fortunately Kim (with her sister Debbie's constant assistance) picked up the ball and ran with it. I did the best I could to help. We were smart enough to hire a wedding planner. But we still had a ton of decisions to make and details to review.

While Kim was doing the heavy lifting, there were things that had to be done quickly that I couldn't leave to her alone, like getting a wedding dress for me and helping her find an outfit.

I wanted to wear a wedding dress—that was never a question. But I didn't want it to be some kind of princess dress—I'm in my midforties, and I wanted it to be age-appropriate. I was open to either a short dress or a long dress. I wanted it to be pretty and classy but not silly. I didn't want to shop for it alone. So I went out with a whole crew of five to ten people: Kim's sister, Debbie; my friend Emily; her wife, Annie; Amy and Meghan (who work with me); and a few others. Not everybody was there every time, but a lot of them were there most of the time. I didn't want Kim going with me to look for a dress, and I don't think she was sorry to be left out of that process.

The first place we went was Vera Wang, where I found a dress I loved. That night I Googled it to show Kim—and found out that Khloe Kardashian had been married in that very dress, at a high-profile wedding, so there was no way I could wear it. I was devastated because that was *my* dress! How could they have not told me that a Kardashian had already worn it? I overreacted wildly, and dramatically took to the bathtub and wouldn't talk to Kim. Clearly the pressure of finding the right dress was getting to me, and now I had to start all over again.

So we went on the typical wedding dress store tour. Everywhere we went we saw lovely dresses and the people helping us were very nice. But at Carolina Herrera the dresses were exceptional and the people weren't just very nice, they were very, very nice.

At each place I tried on more dresses than I really thought possible, just because they were there. It was fun. It was like being a little girl playing dress-up, except that when I was a little girl, I never got to play dress-up. I'd try on a dress, and the group would decide if we'd keep it for round two. Then I tried it on for round two, and we decided whether it would stay for round three. Then from there we'd cast votes and narrow it down to the finalists.

Over the course of several dress-shopping trips, I gained insight into all my helpers and what their personal preferences and biases were. With Annie, you couldn't have enough bling. Emily thought every dress was *the* dress and the most beautiful thing she'd ever seen, and every time I came out in a new dress, she wept. Debbie, who was essentially Kim's emissary, was like the adult in the room. She'd say I ran the whole thing like a meeting, asking one person for her opinion and then the next. But Debbie really ran the show. For each dress, she'd start by asking if it was within our budget. Then she'd say, "Let's turn around. Let's look at that." She'd put her eyeglasses on and then take them off and say "Let's think about this" or "Let's think about that." Thank God for Debbie.

After eight or so shopping trips, the choice finally came down to two Carolina Herrera dresses, and I just liked one better than the other.

But that wasn't the end of it—then came the fittings. Seamstresses stick pins into the dress so they know where to adjust this or adjust that so it will fit perfectly. Since it was a fitted dress, I wanted it to fit perfectly. I'd tell them to make it tighter, since I planned to lose weight before the wedding, but they'd say, "It's going to be too tight!" and I'd say, "No, tighter!" My friend Wayne didn't come for any of the shopping trips, but he came for one of the fittings, and when I stepped out of the dressing room, he wept. He thought I looked beautiful. I thought I looked nice. Not beautiful, but nice.

Now that the dress was taken care of, I decided I had to do some work on my arms. I'd had no intention of buying a sleeveless or strapless dress, because I do *not* like my arms, but I wound up buying a sleeveless dress, and so I was in a panic. To get my arms in shape, I began doing arm exercises with two-pound hand weights—even in the middle of meetings. It was crazy, but I'm not rational about my arms. Then it got even crazier. I began using dumbbells while I was being driven around during my workday. I wound up throwing out my shoulder. I learned my lesson: it's not a good idea to lift hand weights while being driven in an SUV on the streets of New York—while on a conference call!

I gave up on doing exercises in the car, but in the end the weights worked. My arms weren't perfect, but over the course of a couple of months, they were better. My one disappointment was that I hadn't been able to lose weight. I'd hoped that in the final six weeks I'd lose a ton of weight and that at the final fitting we'd have to take in everything. That didn't happen at all—I didn't even lose a pound. So at the final fitting there was nothing to do.

When you wear a fitted wedding gown, you also need to wear "undergarments" to hold everything up and together. As fun as it was to shop for the wedding dress, shopping for the undergarments was definitely *not* fun, especially since I waited until the last minute. At the first place we went—a French boutique on the Upper East Side—all the salespeople were the size of my pinky. I should have known better. The killer came when the salesperson said, "We just don't make it *that* big." The last thing I needed to hear the week before my wedding was that I was too big. I was finished shopping for undergarments and walked out of the store, with Kim right behind me. I wanted to call it a day, but she persuaded me to go to a second place on the Upper East Side called Wolford, and the people were lovely. Not only did they have everything I needed, but they told me I needed a size "small"! I could have hugged them all! Kim remembers me saying, "I will love all of you forever!" to the salesclerks. I'm not sure I said that, but that's certainly how I felt.

Shopping for Kim wasn't easy either, but it was nothing compared with shopping for my undergarments. It had to be a pantsuit because she doesn't wear dresses, and it had to be understated because she hates calling attention to herself. She made clear that she wanted me to be the focus of attention that day, at least from a fashion perspective.

So we set out to find a cream-colored pantsuit that would work with my dress. But we couldn't find anything that worked because it was late February and early March, and almost no white pantsuits were in the stores yet. So without telling Kim, I called one of my friends in the fashion industry to ask her advice. She suggested using a New York designer like Ralph Lauren. So we went to his store on Madison Avenue. This is not the kind of place where Kim and I normally shop, and we made assumptions that the salespeople would be "perfect" and standoffish. But they were lovely! Mary, Cecilia, and Victoria were Kim's Ralph Lauren posse. They were totally normal and nice, so sweet, and enormously helpful.

It was me, Kim, our friend Emily, and Kim's sister, Debbie, at the Ralph Lauren store. Kim was nervous that she wasn't going to find anything, and that even if she found something, it wouldn't be special. But we found a cream-colored suit that worked—the jacket had satin lapels—and to make it even more special, Victoria sewed a gorgeous gold appliqué onto the vest. It was beautiful. Kim bought a pair of sparkly-silver Jimmy Choo shoes with heels (which she wore to the ceremony) and a goldish pair with a lower heel (which she wore for the reception).

We gave ourselves time to decide on our rings. We quickly settled on getting fancy and everyday wedding rings. The fancy rings are simple bands with diamonds all around—I wear mine almost every day. The metal ones are platinum, and that's what Kim wears every day.

I wanted to have a couple of my mother's favorite pins made into hair combs that I would wear to the wedding. They're decorated with white enamel pansies with little diamonds in the middle. The inspiration for using them came from my wedding dress, which had crystals on the midsection, which if you looked really closely were flowers. Also, the pansies fit with our flower theme and color scheme. My mother wore the pins a lot when I was growing up, and wearing one of them was a way of having her memory with me in a happy way on my wedding day.

We had a bit of drama around finding someone to make the pins into hair combs. The first jeweler we tried couldn't get the pins to look like what I had hoped for, but after a last-minute search—and with time running out—we found a jeweler that could. I asked my father to pick them up from the first jeweler and bring them to me. We were having a serious press conference with immigration advocates who were protesting the federal immigration authorities' use of fingerprint records from the New York Police Department to round up undocumented immigrants. It's not usually an occasion for levity. But in the middle of the press conference, my father happened to walk by, plowed through the crowd, and handed me the package with the pins, and I couldn't help but laugh. He knew how important they were to me and was determined to get them to me. So at the press conference I thanked my father and explained to the press that there'd been a problem with the hair combs for the wedding and that we were getting them redone. I noted that my father had picked them up from the jeweler for me, and then added, "So let the record reflect, my father is helping. He wants credit for helping." How could you not love the guy?

We found the pillow for the ring bearer, our grand-nephew Jase Catullo, superquick. I don't know what people did before the Internet, because we Googled "ring bearer pil-lows with a cherry blossom theme," and four hundred op-tions came up—and then we had to choose one! We didn't want to put the actual rings on the pillow, just in case some-thing happened along the way with all the hustle and bustle, so we sewed on our original 2001 commitment rings (so they wouldn't fall off), and our friend Wayne kept the real rings in his pocket. Wayne was very concerned that he wouldn't remember which was mine and which was Kim's because we don't have the same finger size, so I told him to put mine in his right pocket because I'm always right. He didn't like that idea and suggested instead, "Right pocket, because you always *think* you're right!"

We had a lot of fun choosing the food for our reception. It was another team effort—we brought Emily and her wife, Annie; our nephew Jeff; and his wife, Chris. Jeff's a former Auburn University football player, a big guy who loves food, and we specifically picked him because we knew he'd have opinions. It wound up being hilarious, because he had very clear and specific opinions on everything we tasted. He'd say, "This slider, the meat is good, but it's not the right bun; the bun is too puffy, it's overwhelming," or "This would be good if it was half its size," or "This would be good with more of this, less of that . . ." Not surprisingly, we wound up choosing a lot of Italian things, and we made sure that there was a ton of it because the Catullos love food. A lot of the guests were big food people, too, and you just don't want people to leave hungry.

As the final week approached, Kim and I were feeling that wonderful mix of emotions: we were happy and excited and nervous. We only had a short list of things that needed to be done, and all of them were totally doable. Given my Irish heritage, I should have been expecting the potato famine to start at any moment, but I have to admit that I'd totally let my guard down. So when the bad news came, it came as a terrible shock.

CHAPTER 14

Shadows

It was a gorgeous morning, the day before our wedding, and if everything had gone according to plan, we would have been headed to the nail salon or to the florist for a final check of the flowers. Instead Kim and I were sitting in a sparsely furnished and depressing doctor's office at Memorial Sloan-Kettering Cancer Center on Manhattan's Upper East Side with her brother—my soon-to-be brother-in-law Anthony Catullo. Anthony was an identical twin and seventeen years my senior, but since I'd first met him ten years prior, he'd always felt like my younger brother—an irresistible, six-foot-four-inch-tall little brother who was my biggest champion, who would do anything for me, and who frequently drove me up the wall.

Anthony had lived a pretty wild life in New York City as a bartender during the Studio 54 era, and he knew everybody there was to know. After I met Kim's family, he and I quickly became very close. I wasn't the only one who felt that way about him; everybody did, including all the nieces and nephews, who were never happier than when they were spending the day in the city with their uncle Anthony seeing a Broadway show. And somehow he got tickets to every musical you could name.

Just one story about Anthony. He was at the theater with one of his very young nephews who was having a hard time seeing over the person seated in front of him. Anthony folded up his coat and put it on the seat under his nephew so he could sit on top of it. Before the curtain went up, the woman behind Anthony's nephew complained to the usher that he shouldn't be allowed to sit on his coat, because now he was blocking her view. The usher didn't seem very happy about having to do it, but he told Anthony that his nephew couldn't sit on the folded-up coat. So rather than putting up a fight, Anthony traded seats with his nephew and sat in front of the woman who had complained to the usher. Anthony was big—over six feet tall. He didn't confront the woman; he just quietly sent her a message. That was Anthony in a nutshell.

Earlier in the week before the wedding, Anthony had gotten a preliminary diagnosis of pancreatic cancer, and now, following additional tests, we were back for the final verdict. From everything I knew about pancreatic cancer, it was pretty much hopeless, even in the best of circumstances. As the doctor reviewed Anthony's case with us, my attention kept being drawn to the hospital computer's screen saver, which alternated between beautiful scenes of the ocean and snow-capped mountains. I remember thinking, *Why in God's name do you have that running on your computer screen when you're delivering such horrible news? Do you really think pretty pictures are going to help?*

Given that I instinctively expect the worst, I might not have been shocked when we heard the test results. Still, the doctor's words took my breath away, and the implication was almost more than I could take in. While pancreatic cancer was an aggressive disease, he explained, Anthony was a good candidate for surgery—for the Whipple procedure, which he explained in detail using a diagram. The Whipple, in combination with chemotherapy, wasn't a cure, but it could buy us time—months, maybe years.

As the doctor took us on a detailed tour of a diagram of the stomach and pancreas, I stopped listening because I thought I was going to faint or throw up or both. I absolutely could not let myself do that, so I silently repeated to myself, *Don't throw up, you can't throw up, don't throw up.* When I finally was able to focus again, I heard the doctor explain that despite how obviously jaundiced Anthony was, he was not in a life-threatening situation, and that his focus right now should be on getting to the wedding. Anthony made it clear to the doctor that more than anything, he needed to go to the wedding on the following day. The doctor said, "I want you to enjoy this wedding. We know it's really important to you. You're going to be there, and you should be happy."

Everyone we dealt with at the hospital seemed to know about the wedding. Anthony had told us that the day before, when he went to the hospital for an MRI, the nurse who signed him in said, "We all know about the wedding. It's like our wedding here in New York City. We're going to get you to that wedding." Anthony was so proud of us and so excited that I'm sure he told that nurse—and every other nurse and doctor at Sloan-Kettering—everything about the wedding, including details we'd asked him to keep private. And if Anthony hadn't told them about the wedding, it had already been all over the news, so it wasn't exactly a secret that Kim and I were about to be married.

We were a bit stunned by how much press attention our wedding drew, but it had been less than a year since gay people were allowed to marry in New York, and I was the most prominent elected official in the state to take advantage of the new law. On the way out of our apartment building earlier that morning, the doorman at the front desk was reading *AM New York,* one of New York's free daily newspapers, and there was a huge picture of me on the front page with the headline THE BRIDE & THE PRIDE. I grabbed it out of his hands to get a better look. The subhead read CITY COUNCIL SPEAKER QUINN SET FOR HISTORIC NUPS SATURDAY. We'd had no heads-up that *AM* was even doing a story, so it was a total surprise to see my picture on the front—and it was actually a nice picture, which was an even bigger surprise.

As devastated as Anthony was by the diagnosis, he seemed far more concerned about making it to the wedding—and not spoiling the day for us—than he was about his cancer diagnosis. Later, as we were leaving the hospital, he told us, "I want you both to get the family on the phone and tell them what the situation is, and then I don't want to talk about it again all weekend."

But before we could leave the hospital and make those calls, Anthony had to have blood tests. They'd scheduled a minor procedure for the day after the wedding to clear a blocked bile duct, which was why he'd turned yellow. They had to clear up the jaundice before they could do the big surgery, which was scheduled for two weeks later, just after we returned from our honeymoon.

From the doctor's office we had to go to another part of the hospital for Anthony's blood tests, but Kim and I wanted to speak privately with the doctor about the prognosis. We didn't want to ask in front of Anthony. So we suggested to Anthony that he rest for a few minutes while we went out into the hallway with the doctor. The doctor didn't hedge about what a difficult cancer this was, but he wasn't willing to give us a specific amount of time. He said, "You really can't say at this point. We just have to wait until after the surgery to know." And he added, "I'm sorry."

We went back in and got Anthony and walked slowly—Anthony was very weak—through a maze of hallways to the other part of the hospital. Halfway there it dawned on me that I hadn't been back to Sloan since I was sixteen, when my mother had been a patient there. I let Anthony and Kim get ahead of me, because I was feeling overwhelmed and didn't want Anthony to see me upset. I ducked into a small corner of the hallway and began crying uncontrollably.

Looking back, I can see that the experience of being at Sloan with Anthony triggered those old feelings of power-lessness and terror that I had experienced the first time it was clear my mother was going to die. Now here I was about to lose someone I loved all over again, and there was nothing I could do about it. In that moment I was no longer a forty-five-year-old woman who was about to marry the love of her life. I was no longer the second-most-powerful elected official in New York City. I was a sixteen-year-old girl terrified of having to live without one of the most important people in her life.

Kim, who had no idea that I wasn't directly behind her, continued on to the waiting room and got Anthony settled before coming to look for me. After retracing her steps, she found me huddled in a corner near a storage closet, sobbing. She put her arm around me and asked what was going on, and all I could say through the tears was "I'm so sorry." Here she was already dealing with her own pain over the likelihood that she was going to lose her brother, and on top of it she had to deal with me, in a puddle of tears in a very public place.

Gasping for breath, I told Kim how sorry I was for breaking down. She asked, "What's wrong, other than the obvious?" I had a hard time talking but managed to say, "I haven't been in this hospital in thirty years, not since my mother died, and I can't believe I'm here the day before our wedding." And then I began to really sob.

She gently guided me to the nearest ladies' room, where we'd have some privacy. She was very sweet and helped me pull myself back from 1982, when I lost my mother, to the present day. She said she hadn't realized that I'd not been back to Sloan-Kettering since then and added, "I could never imagine walking into St. Barnabas in Livingston, New Jersey, the day before my wedding." That's the hospital where Kim's mother had died when she was seventeen. She said, "You're going through so much. You need to stay here. I'll go back and deal with Anthony."

I didn't want Kim to have to go back alone, so I dried my eyes, and we joined Anthony in the waiting room. When we walked in, we noticed a bunch of people reading *AM New York* with that huge picture of me on the cover. Anthony had already noticed and had a big smile on his face.

Reflecting back on that morning, I feel terrible about breaking down. *I* should have been the one comforting *Kim*.

But once it occurred to me where I was after all these years, there was nothing I could do to stop the tears. That morning I thought I'd had everything under control. All the wedding preparations were complete. I'd stepped in to make sure Anthony was taken care of: I'd found the specialists, talked to the doctors, made the appointments, everything. I was concerned about Kim. I was worried about Anthony. But I hadn't stopped to think about—and steel myself for—the impact all of this might have on me in light of what I'd lived through earlier in my life.

But dark sometimes yields to light, and it did that day. That evening we had the wedding rehearsal and then the rehearsal dinner. By the time we got to the venue, I had pulled myself together. When I practiced walking down the aisle with my father, I was crying again, but this time it was tears of joy.

From the rehearsal, we all went to a tiny restaurant, Piccolo Angelo, in the West Village, which is owned by this lovely family. We were about forty in all in a space that could hold maybe forty maximum. It was very cozy, loud, and festive, and the delicious Italian food kept flowing from the kitchen.

Then our goddaughter Olivia sang. She'd already been on the news because her mom was making our wedding cake, and when one of the local news stations in New York went down to interview her mom, Olivia was in the bakery, and the reporter said, "I've heard about you. You're the one who's going to sing at the wedding. Will you tell me what you're going to sing?" She said, "I can't tell you that." So he said, "Will you sing anything?" And so she sang an a cappella version of "Danny Boy."

Three-quarters of the way through dinner, when we were talking about Olivia being on the news, Kim asked Olivia if she'd sing "Danny Boy" for us. Kim said, "It's beautiful, just let her sing it." So she sang it, and it knocked us all out. And sure enough, my dad was crying, but everyone was crying, including the owner of the restaurant, so he certainly wasn't alone.

Afterward Kim asked me if I wanted to say something, and I choked up again—because I was so happy. But through my tears I managed to say that in my wildest dreams I never thought I'd have a wedding day, that I never thought I'd get to be the beautiful bride.

Then Kim talked, and she said, "I just want to thank all of you. We have such an amazing family now officially comprised of our Italian and Irish contingents." Then she added, "I don't mean to be overblown about this, but we're going to change the world tomorrow in some small way. If some gay child or some parent of a gay child sees this, then we will change their world for the better. What an amazing thing that will be. So as the person who didn't want a big wedding, the thought of making some teenager like me feel that much better, earlier, well, that's a wonderful thing."

At the end of the evening, someone put a Dean Martin song on, and we all danced the tarantella, which is a traditional Italian dance. There wasn't room, but before the song was over, we were all up on our feet laughing and dancing. It was the happy ending to a day that started so sadly, and the perfect way to kick off our wedding weekend.

CHAPTER 15

Wedding Day

The morning of the wedding we got up with the sun so we could exchange gifts before we changed out of our pajamas. We settled in on the sofa with our mugs of coffee, and Kim gave me her gift. Inside the small, perfectly wrapped box was a beautiful rose gold watch that was inscribed "For all time 5/19/12." She knew that my mother had left me a number of rose gold pieces, so a rose gold watch would be a welcome reminder of her. She also knew that I needed a good watch and that I'd see it every day and think of her and be reminded that she wasn't going anywhere despite my worries.

My present for Kim came in a big plywood box that had been impossible to wrap, so I gave it to her just as it was. I knew she would have no idea what it was. The gallery where she had first seen it years before was out of business. Eight years earlier, around the time we bought the beach house, we had passed by a gallery in Asbury Park and seen a Bruce Springsteen photograph in the window. It was a black-and-white picture from 1982 of Bruce in a pickup truck in Brewster, New York. Kim is a huge Bruce Springsteen fan and loved the photograph, but at the time we had recently bought the shore house, and she felt the photograph was too expensive, so she didn't buy it. Over the years, whenever we drove by the gallery, Kim would always comment about how she regretted not buying it. And then the gallery closed.

Luckily I'd saved the owner's card, so when I decided to try to hunt down the photograph, I had someplace to start.

With my friend Wayne's help, I found the gallery owner in Arizona. She had sold the photograph to a friend in New Mexico, but when I explained what it was for, she persuaded the friend to sell it back to her, and she sold it to me.

You should have seen the expression on Kim's face when she opened the box. She would be the first to tell you she was blown away that I'd tracked it down for her. I think that she would have been surprised even if I hadn't had to go hunting for it, but she said that my putting that much effort into tracking it down made it feel all the more special.

After the exchange of wedding gifts, we changed into our workout clothes and headed out for the nine a.m. spinning class at SoulCycle in Tribeca. We thought it would be fun to take friends and family, who were willing to go, to what had become our favorite exercise place. Exercise was relatively new to me. I had never liked to do it, never. I knew it was important, but after playing sports in high school, I had not exercised regularly again until about two years ago. That was around the time I was looking to lose weight, and my friend Annie, who was crazy for spinning, suggested I take a class. So once when Kim and I went away for a weekend, the place we were staying had a spinning class, and we both tried it and kind of liked it and started going to Soul-Cycle a couple of times a week. The short, intense classes fit into my work schedule, and I liked doing something where I simply had to follow instructions. And it's something Kim and I enjoy doing together. Also, the music is very loud, so if you're screaming in pain (which I often am) no one can hear you. And as I came to discover, in addition to helping me lose weight and stay fit, the exercise has helped take the edge off my occasional anxiety and gives me a sense of relief.

It's funny; a reporter recently called and asked to spend time with me doing what I do. He suggested we go out for drinks. My communications director, Jamie, explained that that's not really what I do, so he suggested joining me for a spinning class and then breakfast, which we did. Later he told Jamie, "I give [Christine] a lot of credit, because you're basically just standing there in your underwear with all these people, and they're all potential voters." But *everybody* is standing there in underwear, so to me it's not a big deal. And if anyone recognizes me and comes up to me, they generally want to say something nice, even if I'm drenched in sweat.

Kicking off our wedding day with a family-and-friends spinning class was something we both wanted to do. There's something special about the experience of that kind of class, where you're sort of working in a pack. We thought it would be a great way to bring our family and friends together and launch the day with great music and positive energy.

We rented one of the Tribeca spinning rooms, which holds about thirty people, and sent out invitations to those we thought would be interested, and they wound up filling the whole class. The ever-popular Danny was our instructor. Kim made suggestions for the music list with some wedding songs and other songs that are fun to spin to. When we got there, everyone was wearing a specially made T-shirt that said KC AND CQ, SOUL MATES and the date. It was an amazing celebration and a great way to kick off our wedding day.

Afterward we took some group pictures and then went to Moonstruck, our local diner, where we'd reserved a table in the back room for lunch. We lost some of the group who were worn out from the workout, but the rest enjoyed a cannoli wedding cake that Moonstruck had made in our honor, which was really sweet of them.

We then went over to the Dream Hotel, several blocks south of where we live, which is where our family and friends from out of town were staying. We'd taken a couple of rooms for people to get their makeup and hair done and we'd booked a room for ourselves so we could stay there overnight.

Getting our hair and makeup right took some effort. We'd had a few practice runs in advance, because we wanted to feel good about how we looked and didn't want to have to try to figure it out on our wedding day for the first time because that would be too stressful. Between the two of us, I was easier. Not that I'm easy when it comes to being satisfied with how I look, but Kim is definitely not a big hair and makeup gal, while I've had to get comfortable with hair and makeup because of my work.

For my hair, our hairdresser, Dave, had an idea that was a little "too-too." Then he did something else where I liked one side and not the other. Then he reworked it again, and it was totally there. Getting Kim's hair right was stressful because we had a hard time getting to something either one of us thought was right. One version was a little choppy and spiky. The next was a little too New Jersey housewifey (big and poofy). Kim was remarkably patient, especially for someone who hates to be fussed over, and we eventually got there, and everyone agreed that she looked gorgeous!

We were honored to have Bobbi Brown do our makeup for our big day. Bobbi wisely reminded us that since we were going to have the wedding pictures forever, we probably shouldn't do anything that suggested a particular moment in time, because over time it would look dated. And since the pictures are actually supposed to be pictures of *us,* we shouldn't do something we'd never do. She said we should think of it as just a fancy version of ourselves. Bobbi was very aware that Kim did not want to have too much makeup on. So before she did anything, she'd say, "I'd like to put a little extra x, y, or z on . . ." She was supersweet about it, and Kim was a trouper.

Once we had our makeup and hair done, we were ready to head to the reception hall to get dressed. We had heard that there was quite a media scene outside the wedding space, so on the way over, Kim suggested we drive down Fifteenth Street to see what was happening. It was exciting and curious to see the big press setup behind police barricades, which we were fortunately able to avoid because even though we had our hair and makeup done, we were in sweatshirts and jeans, so we looked a bit silly.

Amazingly I really didn't worry about anything as we moved through the day, except for how Anthony was doing and the logistics of getting from one thing to the next. But Anthony seemed great, and everything went as smoothly as it could (not counting a last-minute panic over whether the tuxedoes came with the right buttons—they did).

Once we got to Highline Stages, our plan was not to see each other again until I came down the aisle with my father.

Kim was going first, so she would already be at the front when I came in. So when we got to the reception hall, we kissed each other good-bye and went to our own rooms to get ready.

The only thing I didn't like about being a bride is that I missed seeing everything that came before my big entrance. So while I was still getting ready and people were coming into the hall, an Irish trio was playing upbeat music. When we were ready to get started, they switched to a slow song to let people know it was time to get seated, and our ushers— our niece Kelley and nephews Vince and Kevin—walked down the aisle and took their seats.

Our friend Maura welcomed everyone and introduced Audra McDonald, the Tony Award–winning singer and Broadway star with the most beautiful voice. Audra has been a tireless champion for marriage equality, and I'm honored to call her a friend. We were thrilled that she could sing at our wedding. She sang the Gershwin song "He Loves and She Loves" but changed the lyrics to make it fit for an LGBT wedding. Then Maura introduced a video Kim and I had made, sort of in the spirit of *When Harry Met Sally*. In that classic New York movie, couples sit on a couch and talk directly to the camera in response to questions about their relationship. So we asked Maura's husband, Mark, who's one of my political consultants, if he could make a video called *When Chris Met Kim*.

The video is divided into three parts. Kim really stole

the show with these perfectly timed dramatic eye rolls in response to things I said. Despite her shyness, she's a natural on film. In the first segment we talk about how we met. In the second, we talk about how we each knew the other was "the one" and about how we bonded over our mothers. And in the third, we talked about our fathers and how the toughest thing about marriage equality being defeated the first time around was our disappointment that our fathers wouldn't be able to walk us down the aisle. I'm told that when the video was shown, there was a lot of laughter, but tears, too. It was probably a good thing I wasn't there to see it because I'm sure I would have ruined my makeup.

Then the wedding procession started, with our adorable grandnephew Jase as the ring bearer. He was followed by the flower girl, our grandniece Jordan. At the press conference right after marriage equality passed, I'd mentioned how we'd be talking about Jordan's dress the next day, at Kelley's college graduation party. We wound up picking a simple white dress for her, with a pink sash to match the colors in our sisters' dresses. Jordan looked so pretty with flowers in her hair and her little silvery shoes—she was in kindergarten at the time. She carried a little basket of rose petals and scattered them as she walked down the aisle.

Then our friend Wayne, who was the best man, and our sisters, Debbie and Ellen, who were our matrons of honor, all walked down the aisle together to "Somewhere Over the Rainbow."

And then from the back, where I was waiting with my father, I could hear the beginning of Kim's processional song, "If I Should Fall Behind," by Bruce Springsteen, so it was time for Kim and her father to walk down the aisle. They were standing in the back where no one could see them. And as soon as the song started, Kim's father said to her, "I wish your mother was here with us." And she said, "Me too, but she's with us, and she'd be yelling at you right now to smile! So let's do it."

When Kim and her father first stepped from behind the curtain, only a few people could see them, but as they headed to the aisle, gasps could be heard. When they came around to the top of the center aisle, the crowd jumped to their feet and began clapping and cheering, which was totally unexpected. Kim says she still gets goose bumps whenever she thinks about it. She was so overwhelmed in that moment that she put her head on her father's shoulder. Then she walked down the aisle to the front of the hall to wait for me. You can see in all the photos of Kim's father how he was standing proud and tall.

My father and I were waiting behind the curtain and could hear the cheering and the applause. When my song came on, which was Beyoncé's version of "Ave Maria," we emerged, and I paused a second to take in the image of the room, which was so beautiful. Our floral designer had arranged huge photographs of some of our favorite images in New York: the Empire State Building, the Washington Square arch, and of course Patience and Fortitude.

It's hard to describe the feeling I had looking out at the faces of those nearly three hundred people who were on their feet applauding. Mostly they were family and friends, and some were my colleagues, including New York's two U.S. senators, the mayor, and the governor. But then I saw Kim watching me, and I couldn't take my eyes off her. She was so beautiful. The amber backlighting against the white walls radiated off her suit and sparkly vest. Everybody said we looked beautiful, but she looked amazing.

It was the first time Kim had seen me in my wedding dress. And in that moment when we locked eyes, I felt beautiful and happy, and I certainly felt loved. About three-quarters of the way down the aisle, I stopped because my legs began to shake, and my father asked if I was okay. I said I wasn't sure. I wasn't sure if I was nervous or just overwhelmed because it was my wedding, but I had to stand there for a moment to get my bearings. Then we walked the rest of the way down the aisle and joined Kim, who was already standing in front of our officiant, New York's former chief judge, Judith Kaye.

Judge Kaye looked so regal and elegant in her black robes, with a red blouse underneath, and red shoes. She was the only person Kim and I wanted as our officiant. She was the first woman to become the highest-ranking judge in the State of New York. And in 2006, when the court ruled against same-sex marriage, she wrote the most beautiful and passionate dissent. She also had a long and wonderful marriage. I didn't know Judge Kaye well, but when she retired from the bench, she was generous in saying that if I ever needed advice of any kind, I shouldn't hesitate to call.

One day I called and asked her if I could come up to see her in her office. When I got there I said, "Kim and I wanted to ask you if you would officiate at our wedding. You're not just on the short list, you *are* the list."

And even before I finished asking, she said, "Yes! Yes! Yes. It's what I thought! It's what I thought!"

Her enthusiasm was so heartwarming. Then she got serious about planning. She said Kim and I should start keeping a notebook of ideas and thoughts; that we should meet to discuss the ceremony; and that we would have to give it time, because she really wanted to make it special. About a month before the wedding, we met with Judge Kaye over dinner. She asked about our families, what we liked to do together, the things we liked to do separately, how we were similar, and how we were different. And from all the information she gathered, she wrote a wonderful ceremony that was heartfelt, funny, serious, and touching.

Standing in front of Judge Kaye at the wedding, we listened as she talked about how Kim likes structure and quiet, and how I like to move at an almost frenetic pace and watch TV to escape. At one point she said, "Kim, you're the lawyer, you like order and law. Chris, you're more chaotic and like *Law and Order*." She mentioned how Kim's dad had bought me earphones so Kim could read quietly while I watched fairly trashy TV. (Those headphones helped preserve our relationship.) And she talked about how some things are so important that they need to be witnessed.

During the ceremony, we had a candle lighting to honor our mothers and the other people we loved who weren't there to celebrate our wedding. Ellen's husband, Bob; Kim's sister-in-law, Terry; and her brother Anthony led that ceremony. One of the candles represented my mom, and the second candle represented Kim's. The third, a large, low candle set between the two tall ones, represented the rest of our family members and friends who were not with us that night.

During our engagement, we had created a tribute page at Memorial Sloan-Kettering in memory of our mothers. At the top of the page, there are two beautiful photographs of our mothers on their wedding days. And on the page we wrote:

IN LOVING MEMORY OF MARY CALLAGHAN
QUINN AND JOSEPHINE CATULLO

In celebration of our wedding and in tribute to the lives of our mothers, Mary Callaghan Quinn and Josephine Catullo, we have created a fund in their honor.

While our mothers will not be physically present on our wedding day, we carry their memories in our hearts each and every day. We are grateful for the time we shared with them and know that they will be smiling even more brightly from above on our special day.

In an effort to further the battle against women's cancer, we have created this tribute fund to help underwrite the pioneering work being done at Memorial Sloan-Kettering, which has long been a leader in the field. Contributions will be used to support research under the direction of one of the world's foremost oncologists, Dr. Larry Norton. We know that your gift to the fund will help save the lives of other women and will prevent other young girls from losing their mothers all too soon.

Thank you so much for sharing in our wedding day and for honoring our mothers with your gift.

Chris & Kim

Then our goddaughter Tori, a sophomore in high school, introduced her sister Olivia. Olivia is an opera student who was finishing her freshman year in college. She sang a beautiful rendition of "One Hand, One Heart" from *West Side Story*.

And then it was time to say our vows, which we had not shared with each other before the ceremony. Here is what I said to Kim:

It is so hard to sum up all I want to say in a few minutes.

I often think that my life before I met you was in black and white and that you transformed it into Technicolor.

You are the most loyal, committed person I have

*ever met. You watch over the people you love like a
lioness and you feel and love at a depth that I didn't
know existed and that lifts me up and inspires me to
be a better, more loving person.*

*I know that our life sometimes gets crazy and has
lots of outside pressures sometimes from my crazy oc-
cupation. You help me remember—in subtle and not
so subtle ways—that at the end of the day the only
thing that truly matters is loving the people you love.
You remind me that no matter what happens in life I
am never ever alone!*

*It is impossible for me to envision a life or world
without you. I can't even think of it. But when I think
of the future with you, my heart warms and I smile
ear to ear and I am truly happy.*

I am so in love with you and so grateful for us!!

And Kim said:

*Chris, I never thought I would actually find you,
but somehow during a time of such tragic loss, we
managed to find each other.*

*Beyond the gift of finding you, I really never al-
lowed myself to believe that someday we would have
the chance to stand before our family and friends and
marry each other in New York. I am overjoyed to be
standing here with you. I know the tremendous fight*

of so many that brought us to this moment, so I prom-
ise to cherish our marriage and to hold it sacred.

And, in honor of your favorite New York City
lions, I promise that I will enter this marriage with
patience and with fortitude.

I promise you that no matter where life leads us,
I will walk hand in hand with you, by your side. And
so long as I live, you will always have my shoulder to
rest your head on at the end of the day.

A favorite priest of yours, Father Mychal Judge,
preached to "never be afraid to love" and to simply
"love each other the best that you can." I promise to
love you, Chris, the best that I possibly can forever and
beyond.

After we exchanged rings, Judge Kaye declared, "In ac-
cordance with the laws of the State of New York, and the authority that has been vested in me by the people of the State
of New York, I pronounce you completely, absolutely and
permanently married!" With that, Kim and I kissed, and everyone was on their feet hooting and hollering. We held each
other's hands and looked at each other for a moment. Kim
had a huge grin on her face. Then we turned and walked
down the aisle holding hands with Bruce Springsteen's "She's
the One" blaring in the background. It's a moment I'll never
forget. I had never been happier in my life.

Tom Duane has wisely said, "Marriage changes nothing

and it changes everything." Before marrying Kim, I remember thinking, *How could it change? We've been together for eleven years.* But it does change things, because it feels like you've added an ingredient to your relationship that makes it more solid, like something added to concrete so it's stronger and can hold up under greater pressure.

When I think about our wedding and consider the life that Kim and I are building together, it still surprises me that I was ever lucky enough to have a relationship in the first place, and that I could be loved by someone special like Kim, and that she would want to marry me. To be with Kim, to bond over the losses we both experienced, and to be in a relationship that's fun and good and one that I'm happy about and grateful for—I'm consistently surprised and astonished. Kim gives me a sense of perspective and support, without which I would have been overwhelmed by the bad moments and given up. And with her, the good moments are even better.

Without Kim I could never have had the life that I do, and with her I am thankful for every day we share, for as long as we are lucky enough to be on this planet together.

CHAPTER 16

Running and Praying

On a gorgeous, sunny March morning, standing across the street from Good Shepherd Church in the Inwood neighborhood in northern Manhattan where my parents got married, facing a bank of television cameras and surrounded by my family, friends, and supporters, I formally announced my run for mayor of the great city of New York. My wife, Kim, stood beside me, along with her dad and my father, and my sister, Ellen. In front of me, holding campaign signs, were our grandnephew and grandniece Jase and Jordan, who were more excited getting ready that morning than anyone (except maybe me). It was a thrilling and happy moment, one of the most important in my professional life to date.

Of course in the brief seconds before I spoke, I couldn't

help but think, as I always do on special occasions when I'm surrounded by the people I love, about the people who weren't there. I thought of my mother and how happy and proud she would have been to stand alongside me. And how happy I would have been for her to be there too. And I thought of my brother-in-law Anthony, who had lived only seven months after our wedding. What a heartbreak it was for everyone that he had so little time! I could picture him standing with us cheering louder than anyone. He would have loved the announcement and the campaign. He would have thought the day was unbelievable—his highest praise.

I thought of Mayor Ed Koch, who endorsed me for mayor two years before the election and even before I had announced. Three days before he died at the end of January, he'd said he wanted to help with my campaign. More than anything I'll miss his spirit, his warmth, and his wisdom from his three terms as New York's mayor. He really loved New Yorkers in ways that I can totally understand. Not everyone agreed with him (and he was never shy about disagreeing with them, either). He made his share of mistakes, as we all do. But he loved how tough New Yorkers are, how unafraid, and how much they care for their city, whether they've just arrived from another country or can trace their New York roots back a couple of centuries or more.

For my family, like so many families who left other places to come to New York, this city was a beacon—a place where they believed if they came, great things would happen, almost magical things. And for my family, they did. My four grand-parents, who arrived in the United States without a penny, sent their four children to college. My parents sent their two daughters to college and encouraged us to be whatever we wanted to be. And that's why I want to make sure this re-mains the ultimate truth about New York City: that it's a place for the middle class to live and grow, and a place that's going to help all those hardworking people like my grand-parents get into the middle class, so they can provide an even better future for their children.

I planned the first day of my campaign so that I had the opportunity to meet lots of New Yorkers across the five bor-oughs and let them know why I've decided to run for mayor. We went from Manhattan to the Bronx to Queens to Brook-lyn and finally to Staten Island. It was the first day of what I'm calling my Walk and Talk Tour, which will take me to every one of New York City's fifty-nine community board neighborhoods over the next six months. My goal is to hear directly from New Yorkers. What's going on in their homes? What's going on in their lives? That way I can make certain that the issues that I'm working on are the ones they're facing every day.

I love New Yorkers and how bold they are. As I've learned over the many years I've been in public life, they ask challenging questions, which they should. And that I'd better be prepared with an answer. During our stop in Queens, one Forest Hills resident had a question for me, and he didn't hesitate to interrupt when I was answering another person's question. I asked him to wait a minute so I could finish answering the first question, and a minute later, when I still wasn't finished, he didn't hesitate to ask again. New Yorkers are demanding. And so am I.

But New Yorkers are also compassionate, and it's important for the mayor to be the mayor of all New Yorkers, whether they live on Park Avenue or have no place to live at all (which we can't accept as a given). When I was in Forest Hills, I met a mother and daughter, and the girl, who may have been thirteen or a little older, didn't seem able to look me in the eye. She asked if she could talk to me, and then asked what I was going to do to help autistic children. This interaction was really remarkable, since her mother later told my staff she has Asperger's syndrome. It was an incredible moment. Here was a young girl who, despite her challenges, seized this opportunity to ask an elected leader how she planned to help other autistic children. I invited her and her mother to City Hall, where we could discuss the issue without all the cameras and fanfare. She said, "Yes, because I'm a little shy, and this is a lot." And I said, "I'm not a little shy, and this is a lot." She must have had to muster a lot of courage to do that, so it was really quite inspiring.

A little bit farther down the block, a woman came running out of the nail salon where she worked. "Oh, Chris!" she called. I went into the nail place, and we found the color of nail polish to match the blue on our posters and literature.

After that I headed toward the back of a pizza place to use their bathroom, when I saw a man in a wheelchair. I went over, and I said hello and he gave me a fist bump. At first I thought it was cute, but then I realized he couldn't open his fist to shake hands. And he really had trouble talking. It took him about six minutes to say what you or I could say in two minutes, but he was so clear about his question.

He said, "What will you do to help disabled people?"

That's where I get my energy: from the people I talk with. Tell me the problem. We'll do what we can to help get it fixed. Government can do a lot to help. That's what we're here for.

My favorite moment of the day came in the Bronx, when a bus pulled up to the curb to let passengers off. The driver spotted me and called out, "Hey Chris!" How could I not respond? So I jumped on the bus, with all the press people following in close pursuit, and talked to the driver and some of the passengers on board. I was quick because I didn't want to slow everyone down. Just before he closed the doors and pulled away, the driver yelled in answer to a reporter's question: "She's got my vote and anyone who gets on my bus!"

A few months back when I was in spinning class with Kim, I had this out-of-nowhere realization that I was the exact same age that my mother had been when she was diagnosed—to the day! I was riding hard, totally focused on my breathing and keeping pace, and it just popped into my head, which was so odd, because it's not like I was somewhere or saw somebody that triggered something. It was nothing like that at all. It was just *there*.

I've heard other people who lost parents at a young age talk about how they had a real sense of this, that, or the other when they reached the same age their parents were when they got sick or died. Until that moment, I'd never thought about it. Never, not once. But maybe I've always been aware of it subconsciously, because I've always lived my life without assuming I'm going to live to an old age, so I have to get as much done as I can with the time that's right in front of me. At this stage of my mother's life, she had only ten years left, and they weren't easy years, but she packed as much as she could into them while her health lasted, making sure that *I* got the most out of life that *I* could.

I don't know how much time I have left. None of us does. But I can tell you that my plan, both short and long term, is to make the most of the time I have—to get the most done and to do the most good for the city and the people I care about. I think New York is a remarkable place that has given my family every opportunity one can imagine and more. I want to keep that going and to make it easier for everybody who is out there trying to make their way through life—to better their own circumstances or to build a better future for their children. I also want to make progress as a person, one day at a time. I want to accept that I can't do everything alone and to remember to ask for help. I want to remember that there is valor in the struggle, and that life's events have an impact on us as people—and that it's okay to embrace and acknowledge that impact on a daily basis. I want to be a good friend to Kim and the best spouse that I can be. She deserves nothing less. And I can only imagine that these are the things my mother would have wished for me and expected of me.

ACKNOWLEDGMENTS

It is virtually impossible to list every individual who has helped me in some way complete my story and this book. That said, the biggest thanks, certainly, must go to Kim, without whom I would never have found real happiness.

Thank you to the entire rest of my family—the Quinn and the Catullo gangs—for all of your love and endless support.

Ellen, thank you for making sure I was never alone.

Daddy, thank you for showing up every single day.

Josh Isay, thank you for your incredible support, encouragement, and friendship.

Wayne Kawadler, thank you, most important for your lasting friendship but also for your skills in interpreting my notes.

Tom Duane, so much of my story starts with you. Thank you.

Meghan Linehan, thank you for always helping with all the endless details.

Eric Marcus, thank you so much for your hard work and for taking a huge leap onto this project with so little time.

Jane Isay, thank you for your sage advice, guidance, and time. I couldn't have done this without you.

David Black, you never stopped encouraging me and kept me going when I had my doubts. Thank you and your team, including Dave Larabell, Gary Morris, and Sara Smith, for your patience and commitment.

My gratitude to the folks at William Morrow without whom this book would not have become a reality, particularly Henry Ferris and his team, Rachel Meyers, Nyamekye Waliyaya, and Jamie Kerner.

To the long list of individuals who I am so fortunate to call my friends, thank you for never losing faith in me and always saying "yes!" whenever I ask for help, and especially for helping when I don't ask.

To the best political team in town—Mark, Maura, Jennifer, Emily (and Josh, too)—and the rest of the posse.

To my City Council team and all of my staff who have made the work that we do possible.

And, finally, thank you to every New Yorker who proudly calls this *great* city "home."